Stillness

Unlock Your True Potential and Find Inner Peace: A Comprehensive Guide to Harnessing the Power of Stillness for a More Fulfilling Life in the Modern World - Discover How to Overcome Stress, Anxiety, and Overwhelm, and Cultivate a Deep Sense of Calm, Clarity, and Resilience Through Practical Techniques and Timeless Wisdom

Lance P. Richards

Stillness: Unlock Your True Potential and Find Inner Peace: A Comprehensive Guide to Harnessing the Power of Stillness for a More Fulfilling Life in the Modern World - Discover How to Overcome Stress, Anxiety, and Overwhelm, and Cultivate a Deep Sense of Calm, Clarity, and Resilience Through Practical Techniques and Timeless Wisdom

Table of Contents

01: Introduction: The Power of Stillness in the Modern World

In today's fast-paced world, it can be challenging to find moments of stillness. With constant distractions and demands, it's easy to get swept up in the chaos of daily life. However, what many people fail to realize is that stillness is not only important but essential for our overall well-being.

Stillness can be defined as a state of calmness and tranquility, where the mind is free from distraction and focused on the present moment. It's a state of being where we are fully engaged with ourselves and our surroundings, without the constant chatter and noise of the outside world. It's a state of being that allows us to connect with our inner selves, our intuition, and our true potential.

Unfortunately, many people view stillness as a luxury or a frivolous indulgence. They believe that taking time out for themselves is selfish or unproductive. However, the reality is quite the opposite. Stillness is an essential component of self-care and mental health. It's a way to recharge our batteries and replenish our inner reserves, allowing us to approach life's challenges with greater clarity, focus, and resilience.

01: INTRODUCTION: THE POWER OF STILLNESS IN THE MODERN WORLD

In this book, we will explore the power of stillness and its potential to transform our lives. We'll look at how stillness can help us to overcome stress, anxiety, and overwhelm, and cultivate a deep sense of calm, clarity, and resilience. We'll explore the practical techniques and timeless wisdom that can help us to access this state of being, and we'll discuss the benefits that come with incorporating stillness into our daily lives.

The first step towards harnessing the power of stillness is to understand why it's important. In today's world, we are constantly bombarded with stimuli, from social media notifications to work deadlines to family obligations. Our brains are wired to respond to these stimuli, which can lead to a state of constant distraction and mental fatigue. When we are constantly on the go, our bodies and minds never have the chance to truly rest and recharge.

This constant state of busyness can take a toll on our mental and physical health. Stress and anxiety are common symptoms of a life that is always on the go. When we are stressed, our bodies release cortisol, a hormone that can have negative effects on our immune system, digestion, and cardiovascular health. Chronic stress can lead to a host of health problems, including heart disease, diabetes, and depression.

In contrast, stillness has been shown to have a positive impact on both our mental and physical health. When we take the time to slow down and connect with ourselves, our bodies and minds have the chance to rest and recharge. This can lead to a reduction in stress and anxiety, as well as improved immune function, digestion, and cardiovascular health. Stillness has also been shown to improve cognitive function, including memory and concentration.

But stillness is more than just a physical state of being. It's also a state of mind. When we are still, we have the opportunity to connect with our inner selves, to reflect on our thoughts and emotions, and to tap into our intuition. This can lead to greater self-awareness and a deeper understanding of our true potential. Stillness can also help us to cultivate a sense of purpose and meaning in our lives, as we connect with our values and aspirations.

In the following chapters, we'll explore the practical techniques and timeless wisdom that can help us to access this state of being. We'll look at the benefits of meditation, mindfulness, and other relaxation techniques, and we'll discuss how to incorporate these practices into our daily lives. We'll also explore the role of gratitude, compassion, and other positive emotions in cultivating a sense of stillness and inner peace.

Ultimately, the goal of this book is to help you unlock your true potential and find inner peace through the power of stillness. We'll provide you with the tools and knowledge to overcome the obstacles that may be preventing you from accessing this state of being, and we'll guide you on your journey towards greater calm, clarity, and resilience.

In the modern world, stillness may seem like a rare and elusive state of being. However, it's important to remember that stillness is not something that can be achieved overnight. It's a practice that requires patience, commitment, and perseverance. It's a journey that is unique to each individual, and it's one that requires us to be kind, compassionate, and gentle with ourselves.

Through the pages of this book, we invite you to embark on this journey towards stillness with us. We hope that the knowledge and wisdom shared within these chapters will

01: INTRODUCTION: THE POWER OF STILLNESS IN THE MODERN WORLD

inspire and empower you to cultivate a deep sense of calm, clarity, and resilience in your life. We believe that stillness has the power to transform not only our individual lives but also the world around us.

As we explore the power of stillness in the modern world, we'll draw upon a range of sources, from ancient wisdom traditions to cutting-edge scientific research. We'll explore the teachings of mindfulness, meditation, yoga, and other practices that have been used for centuries to access a state of inner peace. We'll also draw upon the latest research in psychology, neuroscience, and other fields to provide a comprehensive understanding of how stillness can benefit our mental and physical health.

Throughout this book, we'll also hear from individuals who have experienced the transformative power of stillness in their own lives. These personal stories and insights will provide you with inspiration and guidance as you embark on your own journey towards greater stillness.

In conclusion, the power of stillness is something that is accessible to all of us, regardless of our circumstances or life experiences. It's a state of being that has the potential to

01: INTRODUCTION: THE POWER OF STILLNESS IN THE MODERN WORLD

transform our lives in profound ways, and it's something that we can cultivate through practical techniques and timeless wisdom. We invite you to join us on this journey towards inner peace, and we look forward to sharing this journey with you.

02: The Science of Stillness: How It Affects the Brain and Body

Stillness is a state of being that is often overlooked in our fast-paced and technology-driven world. Yet, it holds immense potential for unlocking our true potential and finding inner peace. In this chapter, we will explore the science of stillness and how it affects the brain and body.

To begin, it is important to understand what stillness means. Stillness is a state of mind and body that is characterized by calmness, tranquility, and a sense of inner peace. It is a state of being that is free from distractions, noise, and chaos, and allows us to focus on the present moment.

There are many different ways to achieve stillness, including meditation, deep breathing, yoga, and mindfulness practices. Regardless of the method, the goal is the same: to quiet the mind, release tension in the body, and cultivate a sense of inner calm.

The Benefits of Stillness on the Brain

Research has shown that stillness has numerous benefits on the brain. When we are in a state of stillness, our brainwaves slow down, and we enter a state of relaxation. This state is often referred to as the alpha state, and it is associated with increased creativity, reduced stress, and improved focus.

In addition to the alpha state, stillness can also help us enter the theta state, which is a deeper state of relaxation. This state is associated with improved memory, learning, and problem-solving abilities.

Studies have also shown that stillness can increase the size of the prefrontal cortex, which is the part of the brain responsible for decision-making, problem-solving, and emotional regulation. This increase in size can lead to improved cognitive abilities and a greater sense of emotional control.

Finally, stillness has been shown to increase the production of neurotransmitters such as serotonin and dopamine, which are associated with feelings of happiness, contentment, and well-being.

The Benefits of Stillness on the Body

In addition to its benefits on the brain, stillness also has numerous benefits on the body. When we are in a state of stillness, our body enters a state of relaxation, which can lead to reduced muscle tension, improved digestion, and lower blood pressure.

Stillness can also help us regulate our breathing, which can lead to increased oxygenation of the blood and improved overall health. When we breathe deeply and slowly, we are able to slow down our heart rate and reduce feelings of anxiety and stress.

Finally, stillness has been shown to boost our immune system by reducing the production of stress hormones such as cortisol. When we are in a state of stillness, our body is better able to fight off infections and diseases.

How to Cultivate Stillness

Now that we understand the benefits of stillness, it is important to learn how to cultivate it in our daily lives. Here are a few techniques that can help:

Meditation: Meditation is one of the most effective ways to cultivate stillness. Find a quiet place where you can sit comfortably and focus on your breath. If your mind begins to wander, gently bring it back to your breath.

Deep breathing: Deep breathing can help us enter a state of relaxation and calm. Find a quiet place where you can sit comfortably and take slow, deep breaths, focusing on the sensation of the breath moving in and out of your body.

Mindfulness: Mindfulness is the practice of being present in the moment and fully engaged in whatever activity you are doing. This can be as simple as paying attention to the taste of your food, the feel of the sun on your skin, or the sound of the birds outside.

Yoga: Yoga is a physical practice that can help us cultivate stillness by focusing on our breath and body. Find a yoga class or practice at home using a yoga video.

Nature walks: Spending time in nature can help us cultivate stillness by reducing stress and promoting relaxation. Take a walk in a park or forest, and focus on the sights, sounds, and smells around you.

Digital detox: In our technology-driven world, it can be difficult to cultivate stillness. Consider taking a break from your phone, computer, and other digital devices for a set amount of time each day. This can help you disconnect from distractions and focus on the present moment.

Journaling: Writing down your thoughts and feelings can help you cultivate stillness by releasing tension and promoting self-reflection. Find a quiet place where you can write freely without distractions.

Gratitude practice: Practicing gratitude can help us cultivate stillness by promoting a sense of contentment and appreciation for the present moment. Take a few moments each day to reflect on what you are grateful for, and focus on the positive aspects of your life.

Incorporating these techniques into your daily routine can help you cultivate stillness and reap the many benefits it has to offer. It is important to remember that cultivating stillness is a practice, and it may take time and effort to fully integrate into your life. However, with patience and dedication, you can unlock your true potential and find inner peace in the modern world.

02: THE SCIENCE OF STILLNESS: HOW IT AFFECTS THE BRAIN AND BODY

Conclusion

In conclusion, the science of stillness is a powerful tool for improving our physical and mental health. By cultivating stillness in our daily lives, we can reduce stress, increase creativity, and improve cognitive abilities. We can also improve our overall well-being by promoting relaxation, reducing muscle tension, and boosting our immune system.

There are many different techniques for cultivating stillness, including meditation, deep breathing, yoga, and mindfulness practices. By incorporating these techniques into our daily routine, we can harness the power of stillness and unlock our true potential.

In the next chapter, we will explore the role of stillness in cultivating emotional resilience and developing a strong sense of self-awareness. We will explore practical techniques for overcoming stress, anxiety, and overwhelm, and cultivating a deep sense of inner peace and calm.

03: The Benefits of Stillness: What You Can Expect to Gain

In the fast-paced world we live in, it's easy to become overwhelmed and feel like we are constantly in a state of chaos. Our minds are constantly racing, and we find ourselves worrying about the past or the future. We are bombarded with information, notifications, and distractions, and it can be challenging to find a moment of peace. This is where stillness comes in.

Stillness is a state of being where we are fully present in the moment, free from distractions and worries. It's a state of calmness and clarity that allows us to connect with our inner selves and tap into our intuition. When we cultivate stillness, we can tap into our true potential and find inner peace. In this chapter, we'll explore the many benefits of stillness and what you can expect to gain from incorporating stillness into your life.

Reduced Stress and Anxiety

One of the most significant benefits of stillness is reduced stress and anxiety. When we are constantly on the go, our bodies and minds are in a state of stress, which can lead to

chronic stress and anxiety. However, when we take the time
to slow down and be still, we give our bodies and minds a
chance to rest and reset. We allow ourselves to breathe
deeply and let go of tension, which helps to reduce stress
and anxiety.

Increased Clarity and Focus

When we are constantly bombarded with information and
distractions, it can be challenging to stay focused and clear-
headed. However, when we cultivate stillness, we give our
minds a chance to quiet down and focus. We can let go of
distractions and connect with our inner selves, which can
lead to increased clarity and focus.

Improved Emotional Regulation

Stillness can also help us improve our emotional regulation.
When we are in a state of stress and overwhelm, we may react impulsively to situations or have difficulty controlling
our emotions. However, when we cultivate stillness, we can
connect with our inner selves and gain greater self-awareness. We can observe our emotions and respond to situations in a more mindful and intentional way.

03: THE BENEFITS OF STILLNESS: WHAT YOU CAN EXPECT TO GAIN

Greater Creativity and Innovation

Stillness can also lead to greater creativity and innovation. When we are constantly on the go, our minds may be too busy to generate new ideas or think outside the box. However, when we give ourselves time to be still and quiet, we allow our minds to wander and explore new ideas. We can tap into our intuition and come up with creative solutions to problems.

Deeper Connection with Others

Finally, stillness can help us deepen our connection with others. When we are in a state of stress and overwhelm, we may struggle to connect with others on a deeper level. However, when we cultivate stillness, we can tap into our empathy and compassion. We can connect with others on a more profound level and build deeper, more meaningful relationships.

In conclusion, the benefits of stillness are numerous and profound. By incorporating stillness into your life, you can reduce stress and anxiety, increase clarity and focus, improve emotional regulation, enhance creativity and innovation, and deepen your connection with others. Whether you choose to meditate, practice yoga, or simply take a few moments to be still each day, cultivating stillness can help you unlock your true potential and find inner peace in the modern world.

04: The Barriers to Stillness: Understanding What Holds You Back

As human beings, we all have an innate desire for stillness, for a sense of inner peace and calm. We long for a moment of respite from the constant noise and distractions of modern life, to be able to connect with ourselves and find clarity amidst the chaos. However, despite this desire, many of us struggle to achieve this state of stillness, often feeling trapped in a cycle of stress, anxiety, and overwhelm.

So, what is holding us back from experiencing the peace and stillness we crave? In this chapter, we will explore some of the common barriers that prevent us from finding stillness and offer practical strategies to overcome them.

The Myth of Productivity

In our fast-paced, hyper-connected world, we are often bombarded with messages about the importance of productivity and efficiency. We are told that we need to constantly be striving to do more, achieve more, and be more. While there is certainly value in setting goals and working hard to achieve them, this constant focus on productivity can create a sense of pressure and stress that prevents us from experiencing stillness.

To overcome this barrier, it's important to shift our mindset from one of constant striving to one of balance and self-care. We need to recognize that taking time for stillness and self-reflection is just as important as being productive. By giving ourselves permission to slow down and prioritize our well-being, we can cultivate a deeper sense of inner peace and fulfillment.

Distractions and Information Overload

In today's world, we are constantly bombarded with distractions and information from all directions. From social media notifications to breaking news alerts, it can be challenging to find a moment of stillness amidst the constant noise. Additionally, the sheer amount of information available to us can be overwhelming, making it difficult to focus on any one thing for an extended period.

To overcome this barrier, it's important to create intentional spaces for stillness and silence in our lives. This may involve setting aside specific times each day for meditation, mindfulness, or other forms of quiet reflection. It may also involve setting boundaries around technology and information consumption, such as turning off notifications or setting aside specific times each day for checking email or social media.

Fear and Anxiety

Fear and anxiety can be major barriers to stillness, as they create a sense of unease and restlessness that makes it difficult to find a sense of calm. Whether it's worry about the future or concern about past mistakes, these emotions can keep us stuck in a cycle of stress and anxiety that prevents us from finding peace in the present moment.

To overcome this barrier, it's important to practice self-compassion and cultivate a sense of mindfulness. This may involve acknowledging and accepting our fears and anxieties without judgment, and learning to be present in the moment without getting caught up in negative thought patterns. It may also involve seeking support from a therapist or other mental health professional, who can provide tools and strategies for managing anxiety and stress.

Busy-ness and Overwhelm

04: THE BARRIERS TO STILLNESS: UNDERSTANDING WHAT HOLDS YOU BACK

Many of us lead busy lives, with work, family, and other responsibilities competing for our time and attention. This can create a sense of overwhelm that makes it difficult to find space for stillness and reflection. When we are constantly on the go, it can be challenging to slow down and connect with ourselves on a deeper level.

To overcome this barrier, it's important to prioritize self-care and create intentional spaces for stillness in our daily lives. This may involve delegating tasks and responsibilities to create more time and space for stillness, or setting boundaries around work and other commitments to create more balance in our lives. It may also involve finding ways to incorporate stillness into our daily routines, such as taking a few minutes each morning to meditate or practice yoga.

Inner Critic and Self-Doubt

Our inner critic, that voice inside our head that tells us we're not good enough, smart enough, or capable enough, can be a major barrier to stillness. When we are constantly judging ourselves and doubting our abilities, it can be difficult to find a sense of peace and acceptance.

To overcome this barrier, it's important to practice self-compassion and cultivate a sense of self-awareness. This may involve challenging negative self-talk and replacing it with positive affirmations, or seeking support from a therapist or other mental health professional to work through underlying issues that may be contributing to self-doubt.

Lack of Boundaries

A lack of boundaries can also be a barrier to stillness, as it can create a sense of chaos and overwhelm in our lives. When we are constantly saying yes to others and taking on more than we can handle, it can be difficult to find the space and time we need to cultivate stillness and self-reflection.

To overcome this barrier, it's important to learn to set boundaries and prioritize our own needs. This may involve saying no to requests that don't align with our values or priorities, or setting limits around the amount of time and energy we devote to others. It may also involve learning to communicate our needs and boundaries effectively, and seeking support from others who can help us maintain them.

04: THE BARRIERS TO STILLNESS: UNDERSTANDING WHAT HOLDS YOU BACK

Attachment to Outcomes

Finally, our attachment to outcomes can be a major barrier to stillness. When we are constantly focused on achieving a specific outcome or goal, it can create a sense of pressure and anxiety that prevents us from being present in the moment and experiencing a sense of inner peace.

To overcome this barrier, it's important to cultivate a sense of detachment and acceptance. This may involve letting go of specific outcomes and focusing on the present moment, or learning to embrace uncertainty and trust the journey rather than obsessing over the destination. It may also involve practicing gratitude and focusing on what we have rather than what we lack.

In conclusion, there are many barriers that can prevent us from finding stillness and cultivating a sense of inner peace. However, by recognizing and addressing these barriers, we can learn to overcome them and create a more fulfilling and balanced life. Whether it's through mindfulness practices, self-care, or setting boundaries, there are many strategies we can use to unlock our true potential and find the stillness we crave in today's fast-paced world.

05: The Mind-Body Connection: How to Use Stillness to Improve Your Health

As the world becomes increasingly fast-paced and hectic, it can be difficult to maintain good physical and mental health. Many of us struggle with stress, anxiety, and overwhelm, which can take a toll on our bodies and minds. Fortunately, there is a powerful tool that can help us improve our health and well-being: stillness.

In this chapter, we'll explore the mind-body connection and how stillness can be used to improve your health. We'll discuss the benefits of stillness for both your physical and mental health, and provide practical techniques for harnessing the power of stillness to enhance your well-being.

The Mind-Body Connection

The mind-body connection refers to the idea that our thoughts, feelings, and beliefs can have a direct impact on our physical health. This connection is not new; ancient healers have long recognized the connection between the mind and body. However, modern science has only recently begun to explore this connection in depth.

05: THE MIND-BODY CONNECTION: HOW TO USE STILLNESS TO IMPROVE YOUR HEALTH

Research has shown that stress, anxiety, and other negative emotions can have a detrimental effect on our physical health. Chronic stress can lead to high blood pressure, heart disease, and other health problems. Negative emotions can weaken the immune system and increase the risk of illness.

Conversely, positive emotions such as joy, gratitude, and love can have a positive effect on our physical health. Studies have shown that people who experience positive emotions have stronger immune systems and are less likely to get sick.

The Benefits of Stillness for Your Health

Stillness can be a powerful tool for improving your health and well-being. By quieting the mind and reducing stress, stillness can help to boost the immune system, reduce inflammation, and lower the risk of chronic diseases such as heart disease, diabetes, and cancer.

In addition to its physical benefits, stillness can also have a profound impact on mental health. Practicing stillness can help to reduce anxiety, depression, and other negative emotions. It can also improve mood, increase happiness, and enhance overall well-being.

Practical Techniques for Using Stillness to Improve Your Health

Now that we've explored the benefits of stillness for your health, let's take a look at some practical techniques for harnessing the power of stillness to enhance your well-being.

Meditation

Meditation is perhaps the most well-known technique for practicing stillness. Meditation involves sitting quietly and focusing the mind on a single point of attention, such as the breath or a mantra. Through regular meditation practice, you can learn to quiet the mind and reduce stress and anxiety.

To get started with meditation, find a quiet, comfortable place to sit. Close your eyes and focus on your breath, allowing your thoughts to come and go without judgment. Start with just a few minutes a day and gradually increase the length of your meditation practice.

Yoga

Yoga is another powerful tool for practicing stillness and improving your health. Yoga involves a series of physical postures, breathing exercises, and meditation techniques that help to quiet the mind and reduce stress.

To get started with yoga, find a class or a video online that suits your level of experience. Make sure to choose a style of yoga that resonates with you, whether it's a gentle hatha class or a more vigorous vinyasa flow.

Mindfulness

Mindfulness involves bringing your full attention to the present moment, without judgment or distraction. Mindfulness can be practiced in many different ways, from mindful breathing to mindful eating.

To practice mindfulness, start by focusing your attention on your breath. Notice the sensation of the air moving in and out of your body. If your mind starts to wander, gently bring your attention back to your breath.

Tai Chi

Tai chi is a gentle, low-impact exercise that combines slow, flowing movements with deep breathing and meditation techniques. Tai chi can help to reduce stress, improve balance and flexibility, and enhance overall well-being.

To get started with tai chi, find a class or a video online that suits your level of experience. Make sure to choose a style of tai chi that resonates with you, whether it's a gentle, flowing style or a more vigorous, martial arts-based form.

Nature Walks

Spending time in nature can be a powerful way to practice stillness and improve your health. Walking in nature can help to reduce stress, lower blood pressure, and improve mood.

To practice stillness in nature, find a quiet, natural setting such as a park, forest, or beach. Take a slow, mindful walk, focusing your attention on the sights, sounds, and sensations of the natural world around you. Allow yourself to be fully present in the moment, without judgment or distraction.

Deep Breathing

05: THE MIND-BODY CONNECTION: HOW TO USE STILLNESS TO IMPROVE YOUR HEALTH

Deep breathing is a simple yet powerful technique for practicing stillness and reducing stress. By focusing on your breath and taking slow, deep breaths, you can calm your mind and body and improve your overall sense of well-being.

To practice deep breathing, find a quiet, comfortable place to sit or lie down. Close your eyes and focus your attention on your breath. Take slow, deep breaths, filling your lungs with air and exhaling slowly. Focus on the sensation of the breath moving in and out of your body.

In conclusion, the mind-body connection is a powerful tool for improving your health and well-being. Stillness can help to reduce stress, anxiety, and other negative emotions, and enhance physical and mental health. By practicing techniques such as meditation, yoga, mindfulness, tai chi, nature walks, and deep breathing, you can harness the power of stillness to unlock your true potential and find inner peace in the modern world.

06: Breathing Techniques: Harnessing the Power of the Breath

In the fast-paced modern world, it's easy to get swept up in the chaos and feel overwhelmed by the constant barrage of stimuli. We live in a society that values productivity and achievement above all else, and as a result, we often forget to take a step back and just breathe. But the truth is, the breath is one of the most powerful tools we have for finding stillness and inner peace amidst the chaos.

In this chapter, we'll explore the power of breathing techniques and how they can help you cultivate a deeper sense of calm, clarity, and resilience in your daily life. From ancient yogic practices to modern mindfulness techniques, we'll cover a range of techniques and offer practical tips for incorporating them into your daily routine.

But first, let's take a closer look at why the breath is so powerful and how it can help you find stillness in a world that never seems to slow down.

The Power of the Breath

On a physical level, the breath is the foundation of our life force. It's the first thing we do when we're born and the last thing we do before we die. It's the fuel that powers our body and brain, and without it, we simply cannot survive.

But the breath is more than just a physical function. It's also intimately connected to our emotions, thoughts, and overall sense of well-being. When we're stressed or anxious, our breath becomes shallow and erratic, and this sends signals to our brain and body that we're in danger. Our heart rate increases, our muscles tense up, and we enter a state of fight or flight.

On the other hand, when we're calm and relaxed, our breath becomes deep and steady, sending signals to our brain and body that all is well. Our heart rate slows down, our muscles relax, and we enter a state of rest and digest.

By harnessing the power of the breath, we can shift our state of mind and body from one of stress and anxiety to one of calm and clarity. We can activate the parasympathetic nervous system, which is responsible for rest and relaxation, and turn off the sympathetic nervous system, which is responsible for fight or flight.

06: BREATHING TECHNIQUES: HARNESSING THE POWER OF THE BREATH

Now, let's dive into some specific breathing techniques that you can use to harness the power of the breath and find stillness in your daily life.

Deep Belly Breathing

Deep belly breathing, also known as diaphragmatic breathing, is a simple but powerful technique that can help you relax and calm your mind and body. To practice deep belly breathing, find a comfortable seated or lying position and place one hand on your belly and one hand on your chest.

Take a deep breath in through your nose, filling your belly with air and feeling it expand. As you exhale through your mouth, feel your belly contract and your hand sink down towards your spine. Repeat this for several cycles, focusing on the sensation of your breath and the movement of your belly.

4-7-8 Breathing

4-7-8 breathing is a technique developed by Dr. Andrew Weil that's designed to promote relaxation and alleviate stress and anxiety. To practice 4-7-8 breathing, sit comfortably and place the tip of your tongue behind your front teeth, touching the roof of your mouth.

Exhale completely through your mouth, making a whooshing sound. Then, close your mouth and inhale through your nose for a count of 4. Hold your breath for a count of 7, and then exhale through your mouth for a count of 8, making a whooshing sound. Repeat this cycle 4 times.

Alternate Nostril Breathing

Alternate nostril breathing, also known as Nadi Shodhana, is a yogic technique that's designed to balance the flow of energy in the body and calm the mind. To practice alternate nostril breathing, sit comfortably and place your left hand on your left knee, with your palm facing up. Bring your right hand up to your face and use your right thumb to close your right nostril.

Inhale deeply through your left nostril, then use your right ring finger to close your left nostril and release your right nostril. Exhale completely through your right nostril. Then, inhale deeply through your right nostril, close your right nostril with your right thumb, release your left nostril, and exhale through your left nostril. This is one cycle. Repeat for several cycles, alternating nostrils.

Box Breathing

Box breathing, also known as square breathing, is a technique used by Navy SEALs and other high-performance athletes to calm their mind and body in stressful situations. To practice box breathing, sit comfortably and inhale deeply through your nose for a count of 4.

Hold your breath for a count of 4, then exhale completely through your mouth for a count of 4. Hold your breath again for a count of 4, then repeat the cycle. Visualize the breath moving in a square shape, with each side of the square representing a count of 4.

Mindful Breathing

Mindful breathing is a technique that involves simply observing your breath without trying to change it or control it. To practice mindful breathing, sit comfortably and bring your attention to your breath.

Notice the sensation of the breath moving in and out of your body, the temperature and texture of the air, and the movement of your chest and belly. If your mind starts to wander, simply bring your attention back to your breath. You can practice mindful breathing for a few minutes or as long as you like.

Incorporating Breathing Techniques Into Your Daily Routine

Now that you have a range of breathing techniques to choose from, how can you incorporate them into your daily routine? Here are a few tips:

– Set aside time each day to practice breathing techniques. This could be first thing in the morning, during your lunch break, or before bed.

– Use breathing techniques to transition between tasks or activities. For example, you could practice deep belly breathing for a few minutes before starting work or after finishing a task.

– Practice breathing techniques during stressful or challenging situations, such as before a big presentation or during a difficult conversation.

– Use breathing techniques as a way to wind down before bed and prepare your mind and body for sleep.

The key is to find what works for you and make it a consistent part of your routine. Over time, you'll start to notice the benefits of these simple but powerful techniques and find that you're better able to find stillness and inner peace in the midst of the chaos of daily life.

Conclusion

The breath is one of the most powerful tools we have for finding stillness and inner peace in the modern world. By harnessing the power of breathing techniques, we can shift our state of mind and body from one of stress and anxiety to one of calm and clarity.

From deep belly breathing to 4-7-8 breathing, alternate nostril breathing, box breathing, and mindful breathing, there are a range of techniques to choose from. Incorporate them into your daily routine and find what works for you, and you'll discover a deeper sense of calm, clarity, and resi-

06: BREATHING TECHNIQUES: HARNESSING THE POWER OF THE BREATH

lience in your daily life.

07: Mindfulness Meditation: Cultivating Awareness and Presence

In our fast-paced and constantly connected world, it's easy to feel overwhelmed and disconnected from ourselves. Our minds are constantly racing, jumping from one thought to the next, and it can be challenging to find a sense of inner peace and stillness amidst the chaos. Mindfulness meditation is a powerful tool that can help us cultivate awareness and presence, allowing us to connect with ourselves and the world around us in a more meaningful way.

What is Mindfulness Meditation?

Mindfulness meditation is a form of meditation that focuses on cultivating present-moment awareness and acceptance. It involves paying attention to the present moment without judgment, allowing us to observe our thoughts, emotions, and sensations with a sense of curiosity and openness.

At its core, mindfulness meditation is about developing the skill of attention. Rather than getting caught up in our thoughts and emotions, we learn to observe them with detachment, like a scientist observing an experiment. This allows us to gain a deeper understanding of ourselves and the world around us, and to make more conscious choices in our lives.

The Benefits of Mindfulness Meditation

There is a growing body of research that supports the benefits of mindfulness meditation. Here are just a few of the ways that practicing mindfulness can improve your life:

Reducing Stress and Anxiety: Mindfulness meditation has been shown to reduce stress and anxiety by lowering cortisol levels and promoting a sense of calm and relaxation.

Improving Focus and Concentration: Practicing mindfulness can improve your ability to focus and concentrate, making you more productive and efficient in your work.

Enhancing Emotional Regulation: Mindfulness meditation can help you regulate your emotions by allowing you to observe them without judgment, giving you greater control over how you respond to them.

Improving Sleep: Mindfulness meditation has been shown to improve sleep quality by reducing stress and promoting relaxation.

Increasing Self-Awareness: By observing your thoughts, emotions, and sensations, you can gain a deeper understanding of yourself and your patterns of behavior, allowing you to make more conscious choices in your life.

Getting Started with Mindfulness Meditation

If you're new to mindfulness meditation, it can be helpful to start with a guided meditation. There are many apps and websites that offer free guided meditations, or you can find a local meditation group in your area.

Here's a simple mindfulness meditation practice to get you started:

Find a quiet place where you won't be disturbed. Sit comfortably in a chair or on the floor, with your back straight and your hands resting in your lap.

Close your eyes, or if that's uncomfortable, soften your gaze and focus on a point in front of you.

Take a few deep breaths, inhaling through your nose and

exhaling through your mouth. Allow yourself to fully exhale each time, releasing any tension or stress.

Bring your attention to your breath. Notice the sensation of the air moving in and out of your body. If your mind wanders, simply bring it back to your breath, without judgment.

Continue to focus on your breath for a few minutes. If you notice any thoughts or emotions arising, simply observe them without getting caught up in them, and then return your attention to your breath.

When you're ready to end the meditation, take a few deep breaths and slowly open your eyes.

Remember, mindfulness meditation is a practice. It's not about achieving a certain state of mind or reaching a specific goal. Rather, it's about showing up each day with an open mind and a willingness to observe your experience with curiosity and acceptance.

Incorporating Mindfulness into Your Daily Life

While mindfulness meditation is a powerful tool for cultivating awareness and presence, it's also important to incorporate mindfulness into your daily life. Here are a few ways to do that:

Mindful Breathing: You can practice mindfulness by simply paying attention to your breath throughout the day. Take a few deep breaths, and notice the sensation of the air moving in and out of your body. You can do this while you're waiting in line, sitting in traffic, or during a break at work.

Mindful Eating: Instead of rushing through your meals, take the time to savor each bite. Notice the flavors, textures, and aromas of your food, and eat slowly and mindfully.

Mindful Walking: When you're walking, bring your attention to the sensations in your body, the movement of your feet, and the environment around you. Allow yourself to fully experience the present moment, without judgment.

Mindful Listening: When you're having a conversation with someone, really listen to what they're saying without interrupting or judging. Allow yourself to be fully present and engaged in the moment.

Mindful Self-Care: Take care of yourself mindfully by engaging in activities that bring you joy and relaxation, such as taking a bath, practicing yoga, or reading a book.

By incorporating mindfulness into your daily life, you can cultivate a deeper sense of presence and awareness, and connect with yourself and the world around you in a more meaningful way.

Conclusion

Mindfulness meditation is a powerful tool that can help you cultivate awareness and presence, and live a more fulfilling life. By practicing mindfulness, you can reduce stress and anxiety, improve focus and concentration, enhance emotional regulation, improve sleep, and increase self-awareness.

Remember, mindfulness is a practice, not a destination. It takes time and effort to develop the skill of attention, but the benefits are well worth it. By showing up each day with an open mind and a willingness to observe your experience with curiosity and acceptance, you can unlock your true potential and find inner peace in the modern world.

08: Loving-Kindness Meditation: Cultivating Compassion and Connection

In our fast-paced modern world, it's easy to get caught up in our own lives and forget about the needs and feelings of others. We're often so focused on our own goals and ambitions that we forget to show compassion and empathy to those around us. However, the practice of loving-kindness meditation can help us cultivate these qualities and deepen our connections with others.

Loving-kindness meditation, also known as metta meditation, is a form of meditation that involves sending positive thoughts and wishes to ourselves, loved ones, acquaintances, and even strangers. The practice is based on the belief that everyone has the potential for goodness and happiness, and that by cultivating positive thoughts and feelings towards ourselves and others, we can enhance our own well-being and promote the well-being of those around us.

To begin a loving-kindness meditation practice, find a quiet and comfortable place to sit or lie down. Close your eyes and take a few deep breaths to relax your body and clear

your mind. Then, focus your attention on yourself and repeat the following phrases silently or out loud:

May I be happy.

May I be healthy.

May I be safe.

May I live with ease.

Repeat these phrases for a few minutes, allowing yourself to
feel the warmth and kindness of these words. If you find it
difficult to generate these feelings towards yourself, try to
recall a time when you felt loved and supported by someone
else, and imagine that same love and support directed towards yourself.

Once you feel comfortable with sending loving-kindness to
yourself, you can begin to extend this practice to others.
Visualize someone you care about, and repeat the same
phrases, replacing "I" with "you":

May you be happy.

08: LOVING-KINDNESS MEDITATION: CULTIVATING COMPASSION AND CONNECTION

May you be healthy.

May you be safe.

May you live with ease.

As you continue to practice, you can gradually expand your circle of compassion to include acquaintances, strangers, and even those with whom you have had difficulties. The key is to approach each person with an open and loving heart, regardless of any past disagreements or negative feelings.

The benefits of loving-kindness meditation are numerous. Studies have shown that regular practice can reduce symptoms of depression and anxiety, increase feelings of compassion and empathy, and improve relationships with others. Additionally, it can help us develop a deeper sense of connection and purpose, and increase our overall sense of well-being.

However, it's important to remember that loving-kindness meditation is not a quick fix or a one-time solution. Like any form of meditation, it requires regular practice and patience to see results. It's also important to approach the practice with a sense of openness and curiosity, and to let go of any expectations or judgments about the experience.

As you continue to practice loving-kindness meditation, you may find that your relationships with others begin to shift in positive ways. You may feel more connected and compassionate towards those around you, and may be more inclined to act from a place of kindness and understanding.

In conclusion, loving-kindness meditation is a powerful tool for cultivating compassion, empathy, and connection in our lives. By practicing regularly and with an open heart, we can deepen our relationships with others, and enhance our own sense of well-being and fulfillment. So take a few moments each day to send love and kindness to yourself and those around you, and see what changes unfold in your life.

09: Walking Meditation: Finding Stillness in Movement

Introduction

When we think of meditation, we often picture someone sitting cross-legged on a cushion with their eyes closed, focused inward. While this is certainly a powerful and effective way to cultivate inner stillness, there are many other ways to meditate that involve movement, such as yoga, tai chi, and qigong. In this chapter, we will explore another form of movement meditation: walking meditation.

Walking meditation is a practice that has been used for thousands of years in various spiritual traditions, including Buddhism, Taoism, and Hinduism. It involves walking slowly and mindfully, paying close attention to the sensations in your body and the environment around you. This practice can be done indoors or outdoors, alone or in a group, and is a great way to incorporate mindfulness into your daily routine.

Benefits of Walking Meditation

Like other forms of meditation, walking meditation offers a

wide range of physical, mental, and emotional benefits. Here are just a few of the many benefits of this practice:

Reduces stress and anxiety: Walking meditation can help you relax and calm your mind, reducing the physical and emotional symptoms of stress and anxiety.

Increases focus and concentration: By bringing your attention to the present moment and focusing on your movements, walking meditation can improve your concentration and mental clarity.

Improves physical health: Walking is a low-impact form of exercise that can improve your cardiovascular health, strengthen your muscles and bones, and boost your immune system.

Enhances mindfulness: Walking meditation is a powerful way to cultivate mindfulness, or the ability to be fully present in the moment without judgment or distraction.

Deepens spiritual connection: Many people find that walking meditation helps them connect more deeply with their spirituality and the natural world around them.

09: WALKING MEDITATION: FINDING STILLNESS IN MOVEMENT

Preparing for Walking Meditation

Before you begin your walking meditation practice, it's important to prepare yourself mentally and physically. Here are some tips to help you get started:

Find a quiet and peaceful space: Choose a location where you won't be distracted by noise or other people. This could be a park, a forest, or even just a quiet corner of your home.

Wear comfortable clothing: Make sure you wear clothing that is comfortable and allows you to move freely. You may also want to wear shoes that are supportive and provide good traction.

Set aside enough time: Walking meditation can take anywhere from 10 minutes to an hour or more, depending on your preference. Make sure you set aside enough time so you don't feel rushed or pressured.

Set an intention: Before you begin your practice, take a few moments to set an intention. This could be a goal you want to achieve, a quality you want to cultivate, or simply a desire to be more present in the moment.

09: WALKING MEDITATION: FINDING STILLNESS IN MOVEMENT

Begin with a warm-up: Just like any other form of exercise, it's important to warm up before you begin. Take a few minutes to stretch and loosen up your muscles before you start walking.

Walking Meditation Practice

Now that you're prepared, it's time to begin your walking meditation practice. Here are the steps to follow:

Stand still and focus on your breath: Begin by standing still and taking a few deep breaths. Bring your attention to your breath and notice the sensation of air entering and leaving your body. Allow yourself to fully relax and let go of any tension or distractions.

Start walking slowly: When you're ready, start walking slowly and mindfully. Take small steps and pay close attention to the movement of your feet, the sensation of your body moving, and the environment around you. You may want to keep your eyes open, but avoid looking around too much or getting distracted by external stimuli.

Focus on your body: As you walk, focus on the sensations in

your body. Notice the way your feet touch the ground, the movement of your legs and hips, and the way your arms swing. Pay attention to any physical sensations, such as the feeling of the breeze on your skin or the warmth of the sun on your face. Be fully present in your body and allow yourself to experience the sensations without judgment.

Observe your thoughts: As you continue walking, you may notice thoughts arising in your mind. This is normal and natural, and it's important to simply observe these thoughts without getting caught up in them. Notice any patterns or themes that arise, but don't judge or analyze them. Simply let them come and go like clouds passing in the sky.

Bring your attention back to your breath: Whenever you find your mind wandering, gently bring your attention back to your breath. Focus on the sensation of air entering and leaving your body, and allow yourself to come back to the present moment.

Practice gratitude: As you continue walking, take a moment to appreciate the beauty and wonder of the world around you. Notice the colors, textures, and sounds of your environment, and feel gratitude for the opportunity to be alive and experience these things.

End your practice: When you're ready to end your walking meditation practice, slow down your pace and come to a stop. Take a few deep breaths and allow yourself to fully absorb the experience. You may want to take a few moments to reflect on any insights or feelings that arose during your practice.

Conclusion

Walking meditation is a powerful way to cultivate mindfulness, reduce stress and anxiety, and deepen your connection to yourself and the world around you. By taking a few moments each day to slow down and tune in to your body and environment, you can tap into a deep sense of stillness and inner peace. Whether you practice indoors or outdoors, alone or in a group, walking meditation is a valuable tool for anyone seeking to unlock their true potential and find lasting fulfillment in the modern world.

10: Body Scan Meditation: Deep Relaxation and Awareness

As we navigate the fast-paced and demanding modern world, we often find ourselves caught up in the never-ending cycle of work, social obligations, and daily tasks. We tend to prioritize productivity over rest, and we rarely take a moment to slow down and tune in to our bodies and minds. This constant state of busyness can take a toll on our well-being, leading to stress, anxiety, and burnout. In order to thrive in today's world, it is essential to cultivate a sense of stillness and inner peace.

One powerful technique for accessing this stillness is body scan meditation. This practice involves systematically bringing attention to each part of the body, cultivating awareness and relaxation. By bringing awareness to the sensations in our body, we can begin to notice areas of tension and release them, allowing for deep relaxation and rejuvenation.

To begin a body scan meditation, find a comfortable position in which you can remain still for several minutes. You may choose to lie down or sit in a chair with your feet flat on the ground. Close your eyes and take a few deep breaths, allowing yourself to settle into the present moment.

Start by bringing your attention to the top of your head. Notice any sensations in this area, such as warmth, tingling, or pressure. Simply observe these sensations without judgment or analysis. Take a few deep breaths, imagining the air flowing into this area of your body and releasing any tension.

Move your attention down to your forehead and temples. Again, notice any sensations in this area, such as tightness or discomfort. Breathe deeply and visualize this area relaxing and releasing any tension.

Bring your attention to your eyes, nose, and cheeks. Notice any sensations here, such as pressure or tingling. Allow these sensations to simply be as they are, without trying to change or control them. Take a few deep breaths, allowing any tension to release.

Continue to move your attention down your body, bringing awareness to your jaw, neck, and shoulders. Notice any sensations in these areas and allow them to release as you breathe deeply.

10: BODY SCAN MEDITATION: DEEP RELAXATION AND AWARENESS

Move your attention down your arms, hands, and fingers, noticing any sensations and allowing them to be as they are. Visualize any tension melting away with each exhale.

Bring your attention to your chest and stomach, noticing any sensations here. Breathe deeply and allow these areas to relax and release any tension.

Finally, bring your attention to your hips, legs, and feet. Notice any sensations in these areas and allow them to be as they are. Take a few deep breaths, imagining any tension melting away.

Take a few moments to simply rest in the stillness of your body, noticing any sensations that arise and allowing them to be as they are. When you are ready, take a few deep breaths and slowly open your eyes, returning to the present moment.

Body scan meditation is a powerful tool for accessing deep relaxation and cultivating awareness. By regularly practicing this technique, you can begin to notice areas of tension in your body and release them, allowing for greater ease and peace of mind. In the midst of the demands of modern life,

taking time to tune in to your body can be a powerful act of
self-care and a gateway to a more fulfilling life.

11: Chanting and Mantra Meditation: Connecting with Sacred Sound

Introduction

The power of sound has been recognized by spiritual traditions around the world for thousands of years. From the sacred chants of Hinduism to the Gregorian chants of Christianity, the use of sound to induce a state of meditation and spiritual awareness has been a core practice in many religions. In this chapter, we will explore the practice of chanting and mantra meditation, and how it can help us connect with our inner selves, and cultivate a deep sense of stillness and peace.

The Power of Sound

Sound is a powerful force that can affect us on a physical, emotional, and spiritual level. It has the ability to calm the mind, soothe the body, and create a sense of unity and harmony. The vibrations of sound can penetrate deep into our being, and create a powerful resonance that can help us connect with our inner selves.

11: CHANTING AND MANTRA MEDITATION: CONNECTING WITH SACRED SOUND

In the ancient Indian tradition of Ayurveda, sound therapy is used to balance the doshas (the three elements of the body), and promote overall health and wellbeing. Similarly, in Chinese medicine, sound therapy is used to stimulate the flow of energy through the body, and promote healing.

The practice of chanting and mantra meditation is based on the power of sound to induce a state of meditation and spiritual awareness. By repeating a mantra or chanting a sacred text, we can create a powerful resonance that can help us connect with our inner selves, and cultivate a deep sense of stillness and peace.

Chanting

Chanting is the repetition of a sacred text, prayer, or mantra. It can be done alone or in a group, and can be accompanied by music or a simple rhythm. Chanting has been practiced in many spiritual traditions, including Hinduism, Buddhism, Christianity, and Judaism.

The practice of chanting is believed to have many benefits. It can help to calm the mind, reduce stress and anxiety, and promote a sense of peace and relaxation. Chanting can also help to improve focus and concentration, and promote a sense of unity and harmony.

One of the most famous chants in Hinduism is the Om chant. The Om chant is believed to be the sound of creation, and is considered to be the most powerful of all mantras. The Om chant is said to represent the three aspects of the divine – creation, preservation, and destruction.

In Buddhism, the practice of chanting is called "Nembutsu" and involves the repetition of the name of the Buddha. The Nembutsu chant is believed to help cultivate a sense of gratitude and reverence for the Buddha, and to promote a sense of inner peace and stillness.

In Christianity, the practice of chanting is called "Gregorian chant" and involves the repetition of sacred texts in a mono-phonic style. The Gregorian chant is believed to have a calming effect on the mind, and to promote a sense of spiritual awareness and connection with the divine.

Mantra Meditation

Mantra meditation is the repetition of a single word or

phrase, often in Sanskrit, that is believed to have a particular meaning or energy. The word or phrase is repeated silently or out loud, and is used as a focus for the mind during
meditation.

The practice of mantra meditation is believed to have many
benefits. It can help to calm the mind, reduce stress and
anxiety, and promote a sense of peace and relaxation. Mantra meditation can also help to improve focus and concentration, and promote a sense of unity and harmony.

One of the most famous mantras in Hinduism is the Gayatri
mantra. The Gayatri mantra is believed to be the oldest and
most powerful of all mantras, and is said to have the power
to awaken the spiritual consciousness. The Gayatri mantra
is often used as a focus for meditation, and is believed to
promote spiritual awareness and inner peace.

In Buddhism, the practice of mantra meditation is called
"Mantra Recitation" and involves the repetition of a specific
mantra, such as the Om Mani Padme Hum. This mantra is
said to have the power to purify negative karma and promote compassion and wisdom.

11: CHANTING AND MANTRA MEDITATION: CONNECTING WITH SACRED SOUND

In Kundalini Yoga, a form of yoga that emphasizes the awakening of energy at the base of the spine, mantra meditation is a key practice. Kundalini Yoga practitioners use specific mantras, such as Sat Nam or Wahe Guru, to connect with their inner selves and promote spiritual awareness.

Mantra meditation is also a common practice in Transcendental Meditation, a technique that involves the use of a specific mantra that is given to each individual by a teacher. The repetition of the mantra is used to quiet the mind and promote a state of deep relaxation and inner peace.

The Benefits of Chanting and Mantra Meditation

The benefits of chanting and mantra meditation are many. These practices can help to calm the mind, reduce stress and anxiety, and promote a sense of peace and relaxation. They can also help to improve focus and concentration, and promote a sense of unity and harmony.

Research has shown that the practice of chanting and mantra meditation can have a positive effect on physical health as well. Studies have found that chanting can help to lower blood pressure, reduce stress hormones, and improve immune function. Mantra meditation has been shown to reduce symptoms of anxiety and depression, and to promote overall mental health and wellbeing.

In addition, the practice of chanting and mantra meditation can help us to connect with our inner selves and cultivate a deeper sense of spirituality. By repeating a sacred text or mantra, we can create a powerful resonance that can help us to access our inner wisdom and intuition. This can help us to find greater meaning and purpose in our lives, and to cultivate a sense of peace and fulfillment.

How to Practice Chanting and Mantra Meditation

To practice chanting and mantra meditation, find a quiet space where you can sit comfortably without distractions. Choose a mantra or sacred text that resonates with you, or use a mantra that has been recommended by a teacher or spiritual leader.

Begin by taking a few deep breaths to calm your mind and body. Then, start repeating your chosen mantra or sacred text, either out loud or silently. Focus your attention on the sound of the mantra, and allow your mind to become still and calm.

If you are chanting in a group, focus on the sound of the collective voice, and allow yourself to become part of the group energy. If you are practicing mantra meditation alone, focus on the sound of your own voice or the sound of the mantra in your mind.

Continue chanting or repeating your mantra for a set period of time, such as 10-15 minutes. If your mind wanders, gently bring your attention back to the sound of the mantra.

Conclusion

The practice of chanting and mantra meditation can be a powerful tool for cultivating inner peace, stillness, and spiritual awareness. By repeating a sacred text or mantra, we can create a powerful resonance that can help us connect with our inner selves and access our deepest wisdom and intuition. Whether practiced alone or in a group, chanting and mantra meditation can help us to find greater meaning and purpose in our lives, and to cultivate a sense of peace and fulfillment in the modern world.

12: Visualization Meditation: Manifesting Your Dreams

In today's fast-paced and hectic world, we often find ourselves caught up in the never-ending cycle of work, responsibilities, and social commitments. The constant noise and distractions can leave us feeling overwhelmed, anxious, and disconnected from our true selves. However, there is a way to break free from this cycle and cultivate a deep sense of calm, clarity, and resilience. That way is through the power of visualization meditation.

Visualization meditation is a powerful technique that has been used for centuries by spiritual leaders, athletes, and successful people from all walks of life. It involves creating vivid mental images of the things we want to achieve or experience, and then holding those images in our minds for an extended period of time. By doing so, we tap into the power of our subconscious mind and program ourselves to manifest our dreams into reality.

The first step in visualization meditation is to find a quiet and peaceful place where you won't be disturbed. This could be a room in your home, a park, or any other place where you feel relaxed and at ease. Once you've found your spot,

12: VISUALIZATION MEDITATION: MANIFESTING YOUR DREAMS

sit down in a comfortable position with your back straight and your eyes closed.

Begin by taking a few deep breaths and allowing yourself to relax. Imagine a warm and peaceful light filling your body with every inhale, and any stress or tension leaving your body with every exhale.

Next, start visualizing your desired outcome. Whether it's a new job, a loving relationship, or a healthier body, imagine it as if it's already happening. Visualize yourself in that situation, experiencing all the emotions and sensations that come with it. See the colors, hear the sounds, and feel the textures around you. Make it as real as possible in your mind.

As you hold this image in your mind, repeat affirmations that reinforce your belief in your ability to manifest your desires. For example, if you're visualizing a new job, you could repeat affirmations like "I am worthy of this job" or "I have the skills and experience to succeed in this position." By doing so, you're programming your subconscious mind to believe that you already have what you want.

12: VISUALIZATION MEDITATION: MANIFESTING YOUR DREAMS

It's important to practice visualization meditation regularly to see results. Set aside a specific time each day, preferably in the morning or evening, to practice this technique. Start with just a few minutes each day and gradually increase the time as you become more comfortable with the process.

Visualization meditation is not only a powerful tool for manifesting your desires, but it also helps reduce stress, anxiety, and depression. By focusing on positive outcomes and emotions, you're rewiring your brain to think positively and experience more joy in your daily life.

In addition to visualization meditation, there are other techniques you can use to enhance your manifesting abilities. These include gratitude journaling, positive affirmations, and practicing self-care. By incorporating these practices into your daily routine, you'll cultivate a deeper sense of inner peace and fulfillment.

In conclusion, visualization meditation is a powerful technique for manifesting your dreams and cultivating inner peace. By creating vivid mental images of your desired outcome and holding those images in your mind, you tap into the power of your subconscious mind and program yourself to manifest your desires into reality. Practice this technique regularly and incorporate other manifesting practices into your daily routine to unlock your true potential and find lasting happiness and fulfillment.

13: Yoga: Moving Meditation for the Body and Mind

Yoga is a form of exercise that has been around for thousands of years. It is a practice that originated in India and has been passed down through generations. The word "yoga" comes from the Sanskrit word "yuj," which means "to unite." This refers to the practice of uniting the mind, body, and spirit through physical poses, breathing techniques, and meditation.

Yoga has gained immense popularity in the modern world due to its numerous benefits for physical and mental health. It is no longer just a practice for spiritual seekers or the elite, but a mainstream activity accessible to people of all ages, shapes, and sizes. In this chapter, we will explore the practice of yoga, its benefits, and how it can be used as a moving meditation for the body and mind.

Benefits of Yoga

The benefits of yoga are many and varied, both for the body and the mind. Yoga is an excellent way to improve flexibility, strength, and balance. It also helps to increase muscle tone, reduce stress, and improve overall physical fitness.

13: YOGA: MOVING MEDITATION FOR THE BODY AND MIND

Regular practice of yoga has been shown to reduce the risk of chronic diseases such as heart disease, diabetes, and arthritis. It can also aid in weight loss, improve digestion, and enhance the immune system.

The benefits of yoga are not limited to physical health alone. The practice of yoga is also known to have a positive impact on mental health. Yoga helps to reduce stress and anxiety by promoting relaxation and reducing tension in the body. It can also help to improve sleep quality, boost mood, and enhance cognitive function. Yoga is a powerful tool for managing mental health conditions such as depression and anxiety.

Yoga as a Moving Meditation

One of the most significant benefits of yoga is its ability to serve as a moving meditation for the body and mind. In yoga, the focus is on the breath and the present moment. As you move through the poses, you become fully present in your body, and your mind becomes calm and clear.

Yoga as a moving meditation can be a powerful tool for reducing stress and anxiety. By focusing on the breath and the present moment, you can quiet your mind and bring a sense of calm to your body. Yoga can also be used to cultivate a deep sense of self-awareness and inner peace. As you become more attuned to your body and your breath, you begin to develop a deeper understanding of yourself and your inner world.

Types of Yoga

There are many different types of yoga, each with its own focus and benefits. Some of the most popular types of yoga include:

Hatha Yoga: Hatha yoga is a gentle form of yoga that is suitable for beginners. It focuses on basic yoga poses and breathing techniques.

Vinyasa Yoga: Vinyasa yoga is a more dynamic form of yoga that involves flowing from one pose to the next in a smooth, continuous sequence. It is a great way to build strength and flexibility.

Ashtanga Yoga: Ashtanga yoga is a challenging form of yoga that involves a set series of poses performed in a specific order. It is a great way to build strength, flexibility, and endurance.

Bikram Yoga: Bikram yoga is a form of yoga that is performed in a heated room. It involves a set sequence of poses and is a great way to improve flexibility and detoxify the body.

Kundalini Yoga: Kundalini yoga is a form of yoga that focuses on energy and spirituality. It involves dynamic movements, breathing techniques, and meditation.

Yoga Techniques

Yoga involves a variety of techniques that can be used to promote physical and mental well-being. Some of the most common yoga techniques include:

Asanas: Asanas are the physical poses practiced in yoga. They are designed to improve flexibility, strength, and balance.

Pranayama: Pranayama is a breathing technique used in yoga to promote relaxation and calm the mind. It involves controlling the breath and can be used to reduce stress and anxiety.

Meditation: Meditation is a key component of yoga practice. It involves focusing the mind on a particular object, sound, or thought to achieve a state of relaxation and inner peace.

Mantras: Mantras are repetitive sounds or phrases used in yoga practice to aid in meditation and focus the mind. They can be chanted or repeated silently.

Yoga Nidra: Yoga Nidra is a form of guided meditation that involves deep relaxation and visualization techniques. It is a powerful tool for reducing stress and improving sleep quality.

Yoga Philosophy

Yoga is more than just a physical practice. It is also a philosophy and a way of life. The principles of yoga are rooted in ancient Indian philosophy and include the following:

Yamas: The Yamas are ethical guidelines for living that include non-violence, truthfulness, non-stealing, moderation, and non-possessiveness.

Niyamas: The Niyamas are personal observances that include purity, contentment, self-discipline, self-study, and surrender to a higher power.

Asanas: Asanas are the physical practice of yoga, which are designed to promote physical and mental well-being.

Pranayama: Pranayama is the practice of controlling the breath to promote relaxation and calm the mind.

Pratyahara: Pratyahara is the withdrawal of the senses from external distractions to focus on inner awareness.

Dharana: Dharana is the practice of concentration and focus on a particular object, sound, or thought.

Dhyana: Dhyana is the practice of meditation, which involves focusing the mind to achieve a state of relaxation and inner peace.

Samadhi: Samadhi is the state of enlightenment, in which the mind is free from all distractions and is in a state of pure consciousness.

Conclusion

13: YOGA: MOVING MEDITATION FOR THE BODY AND MIND

Yoga is a powerful tool for promoting physical and mental well-being. It offers a variety of techniques, including physical poses, breathing exercises, meditation, and philosophy, to help individuals find inner peace and balance. By incorporating yoga into your daily routine, you can reduce stress, improve physical fitness, and cultivate a deeper sense of self-awareness and inner peace.

14: Tai Chi: Flowing Meditation for Balance and Harmony

Tai Chi, also known as Tai Chi Chuan, is a traditional Chinese martial art that has been practiced for centuries. It is often referred to as "meditation in motion" because of its graceful, slow, and flowing movements that create a sense of calm and inner peace. Tai Chi is not only a form of physical exercise but also a holistic approach to health and well-being that incorporates principles of Chinese medicine, philosophy, and spirituality.

In this chapter, we will explore the benefits of Tai Chi and how it can help you find balance and harmony in your life. We will also provide practical tips on how to get started with Tai Chi and incorporate it into your daily routine.

The Benefits of Tai Chi

Tai Chi has been shown to have numerous health benefits for both the body and the mind. Here are some of the ways that Tai Chi can benefit you:

Reduces stress and anxiety: Tai Chi promotes relaxation and mindfulness, which can help reduce stress and anxiety.

14: TAI CHI: FLOWING MEDITATION FOR BALANCE AND HARMONY

It has been shown to lower levels of the stress hormone cortisol and increase feelings of calm and wellbeing.

Improves balance and coordination: Tai Chi is a low-impact exercise that can improve balance and coordination, especially in older adults. It has been shown to reduce the risk of falls and improve mobility.

Enhances physical fitness: While Tai Chi is a low-impact exercise, it can still improve cardiovascular fitness, muscle strength, and flexibility.

Boosts immune function: Tai Chi has been shown to boost the immune system and improve overall health.

Promotes mental clarity: Tai Chi is a form of meditation that can improve mental clarity, focus, and concentration. It has also been shown to improve sleep quality and reduce symptoms of depression.

Getting Started with Tai Chi

If you're interested in trying Tai Chi, there are a few things to keep in mind. First, it's important to find a qualified instructor who can guide you through the movements and provide feedback on your form. Look for a local Tai Chi studio or community center that offers classes.

When starting out, it's best to wear comfortable clothing and shoes that allow for ease of movement. Tai Chi can be practiced indoors or outdoors, depending on your preference.

It's important to approach Tai Chi with an open mind and a willingness to learn. The movements may feel unfamiliar at first, but with practice, they will become more natural.

Practical Tips for Incorporating Tai Chi into Your Daily Routine

Tai Chi can be practiced at any time of day, but many people find that practicing in the morning helps set a positive tone for the day ahead. Here are some practical tips for incorporating Tai Chi into your daily routine:

Set aside a specific time each day for practice: Whether it's first thing in the morning or before bed, setting aside a specific time for Tai Chi practice can help make it a regular part of your routine.

14: TAI CHI: FLOWING MEDITATION FOR BALANCE AND HARMONY

Start with a short practice: If you're new to Tai Chi, start with a short practice of 10-15 minutes and gradually work your way up to longer sessions.

Practice with a friend: Tai Chi can be more enjoyable when practiced with a friend or family member. Consider inviting someone to join you for a practice session.

Use online resources: If you're unable to attend in-person classes, there are many online resources available for learning Tai Chi, such as instructional videos and online classes.

Practice outside: If weather permits, consider practicing Tai Chi outside in a quiet, peaceful location. The fresh air and natural surroundings can enhance the sense of calm and relaxation.

Conclusion

Tai Chi is a powerful practice that can help you find balance and harmony in your life. It offers numerous health benefits for both the body and the mind, and can be practiced by people of all ages and fitness levels. With regular practice, Tai Chi can help you cultivate a deep sense of calm, clarity, and resilience that can carry over into all areas of your life.

One of the key principles of Tai Chi is the concept of still-ness within movement. This means that even as you move your body through the gentle, flowing movements of Tai Chi, you can cultivate a sense of inner stillness and calmness. This is achieved through focused attention, deep breathing, and mindfulness.

In addition to the physical and mental benefits of Tai Chi, there is also a spiritual aspect to the practice. Tai Chi is deeply rooted in Chinese philosophy and spirituality, and many practitioners find that it helps them connect with a deeper sense of purpose and meaning in their lives.

Ultimately, the practice of Tai Chi is about cultivating a sense of balance and harmony in all areas of your life. By in-tegrating the principles of Tai Chi into your daily routine, you can reduce stress and anxiety, improve your physical fitness and mental clarity, and cultivate a deep sense of calm and inner peace.

So if you're looking for a powerful tool to help you unlock your true potential and find inner peace in the modern world, consider giving Tai Chi a try. With patience, practice, and an open mind, you may just discover a new sense of balance and harmony that can transform your life for the better.

15: Qigong: Energy Meditation for Vitality and Healing

In the fast-paced modern world, it can be challenging to find moments of stillness and calm amidst the chaos. We often find ourselves constantly on the go, juggling multiple tasks and responsibilities, and feeling overwhelmed by the never-ending demands of daily life. This constant state of busyness and stress can take a toll on our physical, mental, and emotional health, leaving us feeling drained, depleted, and disconnected from ourselves and the world around us.

Fortunately, there are powerful practices that can help us reconnect with our inner selves and cultivate a deep sense of stillness, clarity, and resilience. One such practice is Qigong, a form of energy meditation that has been practiced for thousands of years in China and other parts of the world.

Qigong, which translates to "energy work," is a holistic practice that combines movement, breathwork, and visualization to cultivate and balance the body's vital energy, known as Qi (pronounced "chee"). It is based on the principles of Traditional Chinese Medicine, which views the body as a complex system of interconnected energy channels, or meridians, through which Qi flows.

The goal of Qigong is to improve the flow of Qi throughout the body, which can help to restore balance and harmony to the physical, mental, and emotional aspects of our being. By practicing Qigong regularly, we can increase our vitality, reduce stress and anxiety, improve our immune function, and cultivate a deep sense of peace and stillness within ourselves.

One of the key components of Qigong is the practice of slow, flowing movements that are designed to help us connect with our breath and cultivate a deep sense of relaxation and mindfulness. These movements are often simple and repetitive, allowing us to focus our attention on the present moment and become fully immersed in the practice.

Another essential aspect of Qigong is the practice of deep, diaphragmatic breathing, which is believed to help us cultivate and circulate Qi throughout the body. This type of breathing involves inhaling deeply through the nose, filling the lungs and expanding the belly, and exhaling slowly through the mouth, allowing the breath to flow out naturally and effortlessly.

15: QIGONG: ENERGY MEDITATION FOR VITALITY AND HEALING

In addition to movement and breathwork, Qigong also incorporates visualization techniques, which involve focusing our attention on specific areas of the body and imagining the flow of Qi moving through them. These visualizations can help us to cultivate a deeper sense of connection and awareness within our bodies, and can also help to enhance the flow of Qi and promote healing.

There are many different types of Qigong, each with its own unique set of movements, breathing techniques, and visualizations. Some forms of Qigong are designed specifically for healing and relaxation, while others are focused on martial arts or spiritual development.

One popular form of Qigong is called "Medical Qigong," which is a specialized branch of Traditional Chinese Medicine that uses Qigong techniques to diagnose and treat a variety of physical, mental, and emotional health conditions. Medical Qigong practitioners use a combination of movement, breathwork, visualization, and energy manipulation techniques to help patients overcome illnesses, reduce pain and inflammation, and promote overall health and well-being.

Another popular form of Qigong is "Tai Chi Qigong," which combines the slow, flowing movements of Tai Chi with the breathwork and visualization techniques of Qigong. Tai Chi Qigong is often practiced for its health benefits, including improved balance, coordination, flexibility, and cardiovascular health.

Regardless of the type of Qigong practiced, the benefits of this ancient practice are numerous and well-documented. Research has shown that regular Qigong practice can help to reduce stress and anxiety, improve immune function, lower blood pressure and cholesterol levels, and promote overall health and well-being.

In addition to its physical health benefits, Qigong can also have profound effects on our mental and emotional well-being. By cultivating a deep sense of stillness and mindfulness through Qigong practice, we can learn to quiet our minds, reduce mental chatter, and develop a greater sense of inner peace and clarity.

Through the practice of Qigong, we can also develop greater emotional resilience, which can help us to navigate the challenges and uncertainties of life with greater ease and grace.

15: QIGONG: ENERGY MEDITATION FOR VITALITY AND HEALING

By learning to cultivate a deeper sense of inner calm and stillness, we can become more adept at managing stress, reducing anxiety, and dealing with difficult emotions.

One of the most powerful aspects of Qigong is its ability to help us cultivate a deeper connection with ourselves and the world around us. By focusing our attention on the present moment and becoming fully immersed in the practice, we can learn to develop a greater sense of mindfulness and awareness, which can help us to appreciate the beauty and wonder of life with greater clarity and gratitude.

In conclusion, Qigong is a powerful practice that can help us to unlock our true potential and cultivate a deep sense of stillness, vitality, and healing. By incorporating this ancient practice into our daily lives, we can learn to reduce stress and anxiety, improve our physical and emotional health, and cultivate a deeper sense of inner peace and resilience in the face of life's challenges. Whether we are seeking to improve our health, deepen our spiritual practice, or simply find a moment of stillness amidst the chaos of daily life, Qigong has something to offer everyone.

16: Mindful Eating: Bringing Still-ness to Your Meals

In our fast-paced modern world, it's common to rush through meals without much thought or consideration for what we're consuming. We may eat while distracted by technology or multitasking, leading to overeating or poor food choices. But what if we approached eating with the same intention and mindfulness as we do other areas of our lives?

Mindful eating is the practice of being present and fully engaged with the experience of eating. It involves paying attention to the flavors, textures, and smells of our food, as well as the sensations in our bodies as we eat. By cultivating a deeper connection to our food, we can not only improve our physical health but also experience greater joy and satisfaction in our meals.

To begin practicing mindful eating, start by setting aside time to eat without distractions. Turn off your phone, computer, or TV and focus solely on your meal. Take a few deep breaths before you begin eating to center yourself and bring awareness to the present moment.

Next, take a moment to observe your food. Notice the colors, textures, and smells. Take a few bites and savor the flavors, paying attention to how they change as you chew. Try to identify individual ingredients and appreciate the different tastes and textures they contribute.

As you continue to eat, tune in to your body's signals. Are you feeling hungry or full? Are there any areas of tension or discomfort? Try to eat slowly and pause between bites, allowing your body to fully digest and process the food. You may find that you naturally eat less when you're paying closer attention to your body's signals.

Another aspect of mindful eating is being aware of the emotions and thoughts that arise during meals. Do you find yourself feeling guilty or judgmental about what you're eating? Or do you feel joy and gratitude for the nourishment and pleasure it brings? Try to observe these thoughts without judgment or attachment, simply noting them and allowing them to pass.

Over time, practicing mindful eating can have numerous benefits for both our physical and mental health. It can improve digestion, increase energy levels, and even lead to weight loss. Additionally, it can help us develop a greater sense of appreciation and gratitude for the food we eat, as well as the people and processes that bring it to us.

One way to deepen your practice of mindful eating is to incorporate gratitude into your meals. Before you begin eating, take a moment to express gratitude for the food, the people who prepared it, and the nourishment it provides. You may also choose to cultivate a sense of connection to the earth and the natural processes that allow food to grow and thrive.

In conclusion, mindful eating is a powerful practice for cultivating stillness and presence in our daily lives. By approaching meals with intention and awareness, we can experience greater joy, satisfaction, and nourishment in our food. So the next time you sit down to eat, take a deep breath and savor the moment, knowing that this simple act of mindfulness can have a profound impact on your health and wellbeing.

17: Mindful Communication: Connecting from a Place of Presence

The way we communicate with ourselves and others has a profound impact on our lives. It shapes our relationships, our career prospects, and our overall sense of wellbeing. But in a world that moves at a breakneck pace and bombards us with distractions and demands, it can be hard to communicate mindfully and effectively. We may find ourselves rushing through conversations, reacting emotionally, or getting swept up in our own internal monologue. This can lead to miscommunication, conflict, and a sense of disconnection from ourselves and others.

But what if we could learn to communicate from a place of stillness and presence? What if we could cultivate the ability to listen deeply, speak authentically, and connect with others on a deeper level? In this chapter, we will explore the power of mindful communication and how it can transform our relationships and our lives.

What is Mindful Communication?

At its core, mindful communication is about being fully present and engaged in the act of communication. It involves listening with an open mind and an open heart, speaking with authenticity and intention, and cultivating a sense of connection and empathy with others. It is about bringing a sense of stillness and awareness to our interactions with others, so that we can communicate with clarity, compassion, and wisdom.

Mindful communication is not just about what we say, but how we say it. It is about the tone of our voice, our body language, and the energy that we bring to the conversation. It is about being mindful of our own emotions and reactions, and learning to respond rather than react in challenging situations.

The Benefits of Mindful Communication

Practicing mindful communication can have a wide range of benefits, both for ourselves and for those we interact with. Here are just a few:

Improved relationships: Mindful communication can help us build deeper connections with others, fostering empathy, trust, and understanding.

17: MINDFUL COMMUNICATION: CONNECTING FROM A PLACE OF PRESENCE

Reduced conflict: When we approach communication with a sense of stillness and presence, we are less likely to react emotionally or defensively, which can defuse conflicts before they escalate.

Increased clarity and understanding: Mindful communication can help us communicate more clearly and effectively, reducing misunderstandings and improving our ability to get our message across.

Greater self-awareness: By practicing mindful communication, we can become more aware of our own thoughts, feelings, and reactions, which can help us better understand ourselves and our own patterns of behavior.

Reduced stress and anxiety: Mindful communication can help us feel more calm and grounded in challenging situations, reducing our stress levels and promoting a sense of inner peace.

Tips for Practicing Mindful Communication

So how can we begin to cultivate mindful communication in our daily lives? Here are a few tips to get started:

17: MINDFUL COMMUNICATION: CONNECTING FROM A PLACE OF PRESENCE

Practice active listening: When someone is speaking to us, it can be tempting to let our minds wander or start formulating our response before they've finished speaking. But true communication requires active listening, which means giving our full attention to the other person and really hearing what they have to say. Try to put aside distractions and focus on the person in front of you, making eye contact and nodding or affirming their words as appropriate.

Speak authentically: Mindful communication is about speaking from the heart and expressing ourselves authentically. This means being honest about our thoughts and feelings, even if they are difficult or unpopular. It also means avoiding passive-aggressive or manipulative language, and instead speaking directly and respectfully.

Use "I" statements: When we communicate, it's easy to fall into the trap of blaming or criticizing others. But mindful communication involves taking responsibility for our own feelings and experiences, and expressing them in a non-judgmental way. Using "I" statements (e.g. "I feel hurt when you don't listen to me") can help us express ourselves more clearly and take ownership of our own emotions, rather than projecting them onto others.

Practice empathy: Empathy is the ability to understand and share the feelings of another person. When we practice empathy, we put ourselves in the other person's shoes and try to see things from their perspective. This can help us communicate more effectively and build stronger relationships. To practice empathy, try to listen without judgment and acknowledge the other person's feelings, even if you don't agree with their point of view.

Pause before reacting: When we're in the heat of the moment, it's easy to react impulsively or emotionally. But mindful communication involves taking a pause before responding, so that we can gather our thoughts and respond from a place of stillness and clarity. Taking a deep breath, counting to ten, or simply taking a moment to reflect can help us respond more thoughtfully and avoid reacting in ways we may regret later.

Pay attention to nonverbal communication: Communication is not just about the words we use, but also the nonverbal cues we give off. Our tone of voice, body language, and facial expressions can all convey important messages.

When communicating mindfully, try to pay attention to these nonverbal cues, both in yourself and in others. This can help you pick up on subtle nuances and communicate more effectively.

Practice self-reflection: Finally, practicing mindful communication requires a commitment to self-reflection and self-awareness. This means taking the time to examine our own patterns of behavior, thoughts, and feelings, and working to cultivate a deeper sense of stillness and presence in our own lives. This can involve practices like meditation, journaling, or therapy, as well as simply taking time to be quiet and reflective.

Conclusion

Mindful communication is a powerful tool for building deeper connections with others, reducing conflict, and cultivating a greater sense of peace and wellbeing in our lives. By approaching communication from a place of stillness and presence, we can listen more deeply, speak more authentically, and connect with others on a deeper level. While it may take time and practice to develop these skills, the benefits are well worth the effort. So the next time you find yourself in a conversation, try approaching it with a sense of mindfulness and see how it can transform your interactions with others and your own sense of inner peace.

18: Mindful Parenting: Bringing Stillness into Family Life

Parenting is a beautiful journey that comes with its own set of joys and challenges. As a parent, you want the best for your children, and that includes providing them with a nurturing environment where they can grow and thrive. However, in the fast-paced world we live in today, it's easy to get caught up in the hustle and bustle of daily life and forget to slow down and appreciate the little moments with our children.

In this chapter, we'll explore the concept of mindful parenting and how it can help you bring stillness into your family life. We'll look at practical techniques and timeless wisdom that can help you overcome stress, anxiety, and overwhelm and cultivate a deep sense of calm, clarity, and resilience as a parent.

What is Mindful Parenting?

Mindful parenting is the practice of bringing present-moment awareness, non-judgment, and compassion into your interactions with your children. It's about being fully present with your child, listening to them without distractions, and responding in a way that is kind and compassionate. Mindful parenting is not about being a perfect parent but rather about cultivating a deep sense of awareness and acceptance of the present moment.

Practical Techniques for Mindful Parenting

Practice Mindful Listening

One of the most important aspects of mindful parenting is mindful listening. Listening is a key element of effective communication, and when we listen mindfully, we create a space for our children to express themselves fully. To practice mindful listening, focus your attention fully on your child, and listen with curiosity and without judgment. Try to understand their perspective, and respond in a way that is validating and empathetic.

Create a Mindful Morning Routine

Starting your day with a mindful morning routine can set the tone for the rest of the day. Wake up a few minutes earlier than usual, and take some time to stretch, meditate, or journal. You can also practice gratitude by reflecting on the things you're thankful for. This practice can help you approach your day with a calm and centered mindset.

Cultivate Mindful Habits

Mindful parenting is not just about being mindful in your interactions with your children but also about cultivating mindful habits in your daily life. This can include things like taking breaks throughout the day to practice deep breathing, being mindful of your thoughts and emotions, and practicing self-care regularly.

Set Boundaries

As a parent, it's important to set boundaries to protect your time and energy. Set aside specific times for work, household chores, and other responsibilities, and prioritize time for your family. Learn to say no when you need to, and delegate tasks to others when possible. This can help you create a more balanced and harmonious family life.

Timeless Wisdom for Mindful Parenting

Patience

Patience is a crucial aspect of mindful parenting. Children have their own pace, and it's important to be patient with them as they learn and grow. Instead of rushing your child, allow them to move at their own pace, and provide gentle guidance and support.

Compassion

Compassion is the foundation of mindful parenting. When you approach your child with compassion, you create a safe and nurturing environment where they can feel seen, heard, and valued. Remember to be kind and compassionate with yourself as well, and acknowledge that parenting is a challenging journey that requires self-compassion and self-care.

Presence

Presence is the key to mindful parenting. When you're fully present with your child, you create a space for them to feel seen and heard. Practice being fully present in your interactions with your child, and set aside distractions like your phone or computer.

Acceptance

18: MINDFUL PARENTING: BRINGING STILLNESS INTO FAMILY LIFE

Acceptance is a crucial aspect of mindful parenting. Children are unique individuals with their own personalities, strengths and weaknesses. It's important to accept your child for who they are, without trying to change or fix them. This doesn't mean you can't provide guidance or set boundaries, but it does mean accepting your child's inherent worth and value as a person.

Gratitude

Gratitude is a powerful tool for cultivating mindfulness and a positive mindset. Take time each day to reflect on the things you're thankful for in your life, and encourage your child to do the same. Gratitude can help shift your focus from what you don't have to what you do have, and create a sense of contentment and fulfillment in your daily life.

Forgiveness

Forgiveness is an important aspect of mindful parenting. Children make mistakes, and it's important to forgive them and help them learn from their mistakes. It's also important to forgive yourself as a parent, and acknowledge that you're doing the best you can with the resources and knowledge you have.

Bringing Stillness into Family Life

Bringing stillness into family life is about creating a space for calm, clarity, and connection in the midst of the busyness of daily life. Here are some tips for bringing stillness into your family life:

Set aside time for stillness

Set aside specific times for stillness in your family's schedule. This can include things like family meditation or mindfulness practices, quiet time for reading or journaling, or even just taking a walk in nature together.

Create a calming environment

Create a calming environment in your home by removing clutter and excess stimulation. Use soft lighting and soothing colors to create a peaceful atmosphere, and incorporate natural elements like plants and flowers.

Practice mindfulness together

18: MINDFUL PARENTING: BRINGING STILLNESS INTO FAMILY LIFE

Practice mindfulness together as a family. This can include things like mindful breathing exercises, body scans, or mindful movement like yoga or tai chi. Practicing mindfulness together can help create a sense of connection and calm within your family.

Be intentional with technology use

Be intentional with technology use in your family. Set limits on screen time, and create boundaries around technology use during meals or family time. Encourage your child to take breaks from screens and engage in other activities like reading, playing outside, or spending time with family.

In conclusion, mindful parenting is about bringing present-moment awareness, non-judgment, and compassion into your interactions with your children. By practicing mindful techniques and incorporating timeless wisdom, you can cultivate a deep sense of stillness, connection, and fulfillment in your family life. Bringing stillness into family life is not about perfection but rather about creating a space for calm, clarity, and resilience amidst the challenges and joys of parenting.

19: Mindful Work: Finding Calm Amidst the Chaos

In today's fast-paced world, work is often a source of stress, anxiety, and overwhelm. It's easy to get caught up in the never-ending cycle of deadlines, meetings, emails, and to-do lists. But what if we could approach work in a more mindful way, finding calm amidst the chaos and cultivating a deep sense of presence and purpose?

In this chapter, we will explore the power of mindfulness in the workplace, and discover practical techniques and timeless wisdom that can help us tap into our true potential and find inner peace, even in the midst of the busiest of days.

What is Mindfulness?

At its core, mindfulness is the practice of being fully present and engaged in the current moment, without judgment or distraction. It's a state of awareness that allows us to tune into our thoughts, feelings, and physical sensations, and to observe them with curiosity and compassion.

Mindfulness has its roots in ancient Buddhist traditions, but it has gained popularity in recent years as a secular practice that can benefit anyone, regardless of their spiritual or religious beliefs. Research has shown that mindfulness can help reduce stress, improve cognitive function, boost creativity, and enhance overall well-being.

How can Mindfulness Help in the Workplace?

Given its many benefits, it's not surprising that mindfulness has become increasingly popular in the workplace. From Silicon Valley tech giants to traditional corporations, companies are recognizing the value of mindfulness as a tool for improving employee performance, reducing burnout, and fostering a more positive work culture.

Some of the specific ways in which mindfulness can benefit employees and organizations include:

Increased focus and productivity: By learning to stay present and focused, employees can get more done in less time, without getting distracted by irrelevant thoughts or external stimuli.

Better decision-making: Mindfulness can help employees approach problems with clarity and objectivity, allowing them to make better decisions that are not clouded by biases or emotions.

Improved communication: Mindfulness can help employees listen more effectively, express themselves more clearly, and cultivate deeper connections with their colleagues.

Reduced stress and burnout: Mindfulness can help employees manage their stress levels and avoid burnout, by teaching them to recognize and respond to the signs of stress in a healthy way.

Increased creativity and innovation: By cultivating a more open and receptive state of mind, employees can tap into their creative potential and come up with innovative solutions to problems.

Practical Techniques for Mindful Work

So how can we cultivate mindfulness in the workplace? Here are some practical techniques and exercises that you can try:

Mindful breathing: One of the simplest and most effective ways to cultivate mindfulness is through mindful breathing.

Take a few moments to focus on your breath, noticing the sensation of the air moving in and out of your body. If your mind wanders, gently bring it back to your breath.

Body scan: Another mindfulness practice that can be done at work is the body scan. Close your eyes and bring your attention to different parts of your body, starting with your feet and moving up to your head. Notice any sensations, without judgment or interpretation.

Mindful listening: When in a meeting or conversation, practice mindful listening by giving the other person your full attention. Resist the urge to interrupt or prepare your response, and instead focus on really hearing what they are saying.

Mindful walking: Take a break from your desk and go for a mindful walk. Pay attention to the sensation of your feet touching the ground, the movement of your body, and the sights and sounds around you.

Mindful eating: When you eat your lunch or snacks, take a few moments to really savor the flavors and textures of the food. Notice the sensations in your mouth and the feelings of hunger and fullness in your body.

Timeless Wisdom for Mindful Work

In addition to these practical techniques, there are also many timeless teachings and philosophies that can help us cultivate a more mindful approach to work. Here are a few examples:

The Power of Presence: In his book, "The Power of Now," spiritual teacher Eckhart Tolle emphasizes the importance of being fully present in the moment. He writes, "Realize deeply that the present moment is all you ever have. Make the Now the primary focus of your life." By cultivating a deep sense of presence, we can approach our work with greater focus, clarity, and purpose.

The Art of Flow: Psychologist Mihaly Csikszentmihalyi has written extensively on the concept of flow, which refers to a state of optimal experience where we are fully engaged in an activity and lose track of time. By finding activities that challenge us but also match our skills, we can enter a state of flow that can help us achieve greater productivity, creativity, and satisfaction at work.

19: MINDFUL WORK: FINDING CALM AMIDST THE CHAOS

The Value of Compassion: Compassion is an essential component of mindfulness, as it allows us to approach ourselves and others with kindness and understanding. In his book, "The Book of Joy," the Dalai Lama writes, "If you want others to be happy, practice compassion. If you want to be happy, practice compassion." By cultivating compassion for ourselves and our colleagues, we can create a more supportive and positive work environment.

The Importance of Purpose: Having a sense of purpose and meaning in our work can help us stay motivated and engaged, even during challenging times. In his book, "Drive," author Daniel Pink argues that people are most motivated when they have autonomy, mastery, and purpose in their work. By finding ways to connect our work to a larger sense of purpose, we can stay inspired and committed to our goals.

Conclusion

Mindful work is not just a buzzword or a passing trend - it's a powerful tool for unlocking our true potential and finding inner peace in the modern world. By cultivating mindfulness in the workplace, we can reduce stress and overwhelm, improve our productivity and creativity, and foster a more positive and supportive work culture. Whether through practical techniques or timeless wisdom, there are many ways to bring more mindfulness to our work and create a more fulfilling and satisfying career.

20: Mindful Technology: Using Devices with Awareness

The modern world has made technology an integral part of our daily lives. From smartphones to laptops, we are constantly connected to the digital world. While technology has brought many benefits, it has also brought new challenges. The constant notifications, emails, and social media updates can lead to distraction and overwhelm, making it harder to find stillness and inner peace. In this chapter, we will explore how to use technology mindfully and in a way that supports our well-being.

The first step towards using technology mindfully is to recognize the impact it has on our mental and emotional states. When we are constantly checking our devices, we are interrupting our focus and attention, and preventing ourselves from fully engaging in the present moment. This can lead to feelings of stress, anxiety, and a sense of being overwhelmed. It's important to take breaks from technology throughout the day, and to be intentional about how we use our devices.

One technique for using technology mindfully is to set boundaries and create a schedule. This means setting specific times during the day to check email, social media, and other notifications. By doing so, we can minimize distractions and regain control over our attention. We can also turn off notifications and use apps that help us stay focused, such as time-tracking apps or apps that limit our usage.

Another technique is to practice mindfulness while using technology. This means being fully present and aware of our thoughts and emotions as we engage with our devices. We can practice mindfulness by taking a few deep breaths before checking our phone or computer, and by checking in with ourselves regularly to see how we are feeling. We can also set an intention for how we want to use our device before we start, such as "I will use my phone to connect with loved ones" or "I will use my laptop to work on a specific task."

It's also important to create healthy habits around technology use. This means taking care of our physical health by ensuring we get enough sleep, exercise, and breaks throughout the day. We can also create boundaries around our technology use by setting limits on how much time we spend on our devices each day. This can help us cultivate a sense of balance and prevent burnout.

Finally, we can use technology in a way that supports our well-being. There are many apps and tools available that can help us cultivate mindfulness, reduce stress, and promote relaxation. These include meditation apps, yoga apps, and apps that help us track our sleep and exercise. By using technology in a way that supports our well-being, we can turn it into a tool for personal growth and development.

In conclusion, technology is a powerful tool that has the potential to both support and detract from our well-being. By using it mindfully and intentionally, we can minimize its negative effects and harness its power to support our growth and development. By setting boundaries, practicing mindfulness, creating healthy habits, and using technology to support our well-being, we can find greater stillness, inner peace, and resilience in the modern world.

21: Digital Detox: Disconnecting to Reconnect with Yourself

In our modern world, we are constantly bombarded with a deluge of information and stimulation, all vying for our attention. From social media updates and news alerts to emails and text messages, we are always connected, always plugged in, always on. This constant state of digital hyperactivity can be overwhelming, exhausting, and ultimately detrimental to our health and well-being.

It's no wonder that more and more people are turning to the practice of digital detoxing, where they disconnect from technology and reconnect with themselves and the world around them. In this chapter, we'll explore the benefits of digital detoxing, the different approaches to a digital detox, and practical tips for how to implement a successful digital detox.

Benefits of Digital Detoxing

The benefits of digital detoxing are numerous and well-documented. Here are just a few of the ways that a digital detox can positively impact your life:

Reduced Stress and Anxiety: The constant barrage of notifications, updates, and messages can leave us feeling overwhelmed and anxious. Digital detoxing allows us to step away from the noise and give our minds a much-needed break.

Increased Focus and Productivity: When we're not constantly distracted by our devices, we're able to concentrate more fully on the task at hand, which can lead to increased productivity and better results.

Improved Sleep: The blue light emitted by screens can disrupt our circadian rhythms and make it harder to fall asleep. By disconnecting from technology before bed, we can improve the quality of our sleep and wake up feeling more refreshed.

Stronger Relationships: When we're not constantly checking our phones or scrolling through social media, we can be more present and attentive to the people in our lives, which can strengthen our relationships and improve our connections with others.

Greater Self-Awareness: By disconnecting from technology

and tuning into our own thoughts and feelings, we can gain a deeper understanding of ourselves and our place in the world, which can lead to greater self-awareness and personal growth.

Approaches to Digital Detoxing

There are many different approaches to digital detoxing, and the right one for you will depend on your lifestyle, preferences, and goals. Here are a few options to consider:

Cold Turkey: This approach involves completely cutting off all technology for a set period of time, such as a weekend or a week-long retreat. While this can be challenging, it can also be the most effective way to fully disconnect and reset.

Gradual Reduction: This approach involves slowly reducing your technology use over time, such as by setting aside certain hours of the day when you won't check your phone or email. This can be a good option for those who need to stay connected for work or other reasons.

Digital Sabbaticals: This approach involves taking regular breaks from technology, such as by unplugging for a day or two each week or going on a digital detox vacation. This can be a good way to make digital detoxing a regular part of your routine.

Tips for a Successful Digital Detox

Regardless of which approach you choose, here are some practical tips for how to implement a successful digital detox:

Set Clear Boundaries: Decide on the specific rules and guidelines for your digital detox and communicate them to the people in your life who may be affected. This can help you stick to your plan and avoid any confusion or conflict.

Find Alternative Activities: Make a list of activities you can do instead of using technology, such as reading, hiking, or spending time with friends and family. This can help you stay engaged and avoid the temptation to check your phone.

Be Prepared for Withdrawal: Going without technology can be challenging, especially at first. Be prepared for feelings of withdrawal or discomfort, and have a plan for how to cope with them. This might include practicing mindfulness or meditation, spending time in nature, or engaging in physical activity.

Set Realistic Goals: Don't try to completely overhaul your digital habits overnight. Set realistic goals for your digital detox and celebrate small victories along the way.

Be Mindful of Triggers: Pay attention to the situations or emotions that trigger your technology use, such as boredom or anxiety. Once you identify these triggers, you can develop strategies for how to cope with them without turning to your devices.

Build Accountability: Having a support system can be a powerful motivator for sticking to your digital detox. Consider recruiting a friend or family member to join you in your detox, or sharing your progress with a support group or online community.

Reflect on Your Experience: After your digital detox is complete, take some time to reflect on your experience. What did you learn about yourself? What benefits did you experience? What challenges did you face? This reflection can help you identify what worked well and what areas you may want to improve upon for your next digital detox.

Conclusion

Digital detoxing can be a powerful tool for cultivating inner stillness, improving well-being, and enhancing our relationships with others. By disconnecting from technology and tuning into ourselves and the world around us, we can tap into a deep sense of calm, clarity, and resilience that can help us navigate the challenges of modern life with greater ease and grace. Whether you choose to go cold turkey or take a more gradual approach, a digital detox can be a transformative experience that unlocks your true potential and helps you live a more fulfilling life.

22: Nature Connection: Finding Stillness in the Natural World

Introduction:

The world we live in today is fast-paced, chaotic, and overwhelming. We are constantly bombarded with stimuli from every direction, and it can be challenging to find a moment of peace amidst the chaos. However, there is a remedy for this: connecting with nature. In this chapter, we will explore how nature can help us find stillness in our lives and how we can cultivate a deeper connection with the natural world.

Part 1: The Power of Nature Connection

There is no denying the power of nature. For centuries, people have turned to the natural world for healing, solace, and guidance. From the ancient Greeks to the Native Americans, people have recognized the importance of connecting with nature for physical, emotional, and spiritual well-being. Modern science has also confirmed the many benefits of nature connection.

Research shows that spending time in nature can reduce stress, anxiety, and depression, improve immune function, lower blood pressure, and increase creativity and cognitive function. Additionally, studies have found that exposure to natural environments can improve our mood, boost our self-esteem, and enhance our sense of purpose and meaning in life.

The reason nature is so powerful is that it provides us with a sense of stillness that is hard to find in our modern world. When we are in nature, we can disconnect from the distractions of technology and the stress of daily life. We can quiet our minds and connect with something larger than ourselves, which can help us gain perspective and clarity.

Part 2: How to Connect with Nature

Connecting with nature is not difficult, but it does require intention and mindfulness. Here are some ways you can cultivate a deeper connection with the natural world:

Spend time in nature: The simplest way to connect with nature is to spend time in it. This could be a walk in the park, a hike in the mountains, or a swim in the ocean. It doesn't matter what you do; what matters is that you are present and engaged with the natural world around you.

22: NATURE CONNECTION: FINDING STILLNESS IN THE NATURAL WORLD

Practice mindfulness: Mindfulness is the practice of being present in the moment, without judgment. When you are in nature, practice mindfulness by observing your surroundings with curiosity and openness. Notice the colors, textures, and sounds around you. Take deep breaths and feel the air on your skin. Allow yourself to fully experience the moment.

Engage your senses: Our senses are our connection to the world around us. When we engage our senses, we become more present and alive. In nature, engage your senses by smelling the flowers, feeling the grass under your feet, and listening to the birds. Take a moment to really savor the experience.

Meditate in nature: Meditation is a powerful tool for finding stillness and inner peace. When you meditate in nature, you can deepen your connection with the natural world while also calming your mind. Find a quiet spot in nature and sit comfortably. Close your eyes and focus on your breath. Allow yourself to be still and present in the moment.

Part 3: Cultivating a Deeper Connection with Nature

22: NATURE CONNECTION: FINDING STILLNESS IN THE NATURAL WORLD

Connecting with nature is a lifelong practice. Here are some ways you can cultivate a deeper connection with the natural world over time:

Learn about nature: The more you know about nature, the more you will appreciate it. Take the time to learn about the plants, animals, and ecosystems around you. Read books, watch documentaries, and take classes. The more you understand, the more you will see the interconnectedness of all things.

Practice gratitude: Gratitude is the practice of recognizing the good in your life. When you practice gratitude for nature, you will begin to see the beauty and wonder in the world around you. Take a moment each day to reflect on something in nature that you are grateful for.

Make nature a part of your daily life: Finding stillness in nature doesn't have to be a special occasion. You can make nature a part of your daily routine by incorporating it into your life. This could be as simple as taking a walk in a nearby park or adding a plant to your workspace. By making nature a regular part of your life, you will be more likely to find stillness and peace in your daily routine.

22: NATURE CONNECTION: FINDING STILLNESS IN THE NATURAL WORLD

Volunteer for environmental causes: Volunteering for environmental causes is a great way to give back to nature while also deepening your connection with it. Whether it's participating in a beach clean-up or volunteering at a local conservation organization, getting involved in environmental causes can help you feel more connected to the natural world.

Practice sustainable living: Living sustainably is an important way to honor and respect the natural world. By reducing your carbon footprint, conserving resources, and making eco-friendly choices, you can live in a way that supports the health and well-being of the planet. When you live sustainably, you are also deepening your connection with nature by recognizing the interconnectedness of all things.

Conclusion:

Connecting with nature is a powerful way to find stillness and inner peace in the modern world. By spending time in nature, practicing mindfulness, engaging your senses, and meditating, you can cultivate a deeper connection with the natural world. And by learning about nature, practicing gratitude, making nature a part of your daily life, volunteer-

ing for environmental causes, and practicing sustainable living, you can deepen that connection even further. So go outside, breathe in the fresh air, and find stillness in the beauty
and wonder of the natural world.

23: Art and Creativity: Finding Stillness in Expression

Art and creativity are powerful vehicles for stillness. They offer a way to tap into the present moment, to connect with something greater than ourselves, and to find meaning and purpose in our lives. In this chapter, we explore the transformative power of art and creativity and how they can help us cultivate stillness in our lives.

The Power of Art

Art has been an essential part of human expression for thousands of years. From the earliest cave paintings to the great works of the Renaissance and beyond, art has captured the imagination and inspired countless generations. But what is it about art that makes it so powerful?

At its core, art is about communication. It's a way to express ideas, emotions, and experiences that can't be captured in words. Art has the power to move us, to challenge us, and to make us see the world in a new way.

One of the most potent aspects of art is its ability to evoke stillness. When we look at a piece of art, we enter into a state of contemplation. We're drawn into the present moment, and all distractions fall away. For that moment, we're completely absorbed in the artwork, and everything else fades into the background.

Art can also be a catalyst for personal growth and transformation. By exploring different art forms and styles, we can connect with our innermost selves and uncover hidden talents and passions. Art can help us develop empathy and compassion, as we gain a deeper understanding of the human experience.

The Power of Creativity

Creativity is often thought of as a mysterious and elusive quality. But in reality, creativity is something that we all possess. It's the ability to connect seemingly unrelated ideas and to see things in a new way. And just like art, creativity has the power to bring us into the present moment and help us find stillness.

When we're engaged in a creative pursuit, whether it's writing, painting, or cooking, we're completely absorbed in the task at hand. We're not thinking about the past or worrying about the future. We're fully present, in a state of flow.

Studies have shown that creativity can have numerous benefits for our mental and emotional well-being. It can reduce stress and anxiety, improve mood, and increase our sense of self-worth. When we create, we tap into our innate creativity and discover new aspects of ourselves.

Finding Stillness in Art and Creativity

So how can we use art and creativity to cultivate stillness in our lives? There are many different ways to approach this, but here are a few ideas to get you started:

Practice Mindful Art: Mindful art is a form of meditation that involves creating art in a focused, non-judgmental way. It's about being fully present in the moment, without worrying about the outcome. You can try mindful drawing, painting, or even coloring in a coloring book. The goal is to engage in the creative process without any expectations or pressure.

Explore Different Art Forms: Trying out different art forms can help you discover new ways of expressing yourself and tapping into your creativity. Consider taking a pottery class, trying your hand at photography, or learning how to play an instrument. The possibilities are endless.

Make Time for Creativity: It's easy to get caught up in the busyness of everyday life and forget to make time for creativity. But setting aside dedicated time for creative pursuits can help you cultivate stillness and tap into your innermost self. Whether it's 30 minutes a day or a few hours a week, make a commitment to prioritize creativity in your life.

Practice Playfulness: Sometimes we can get too caught up in the idea of creating something "perfect." But creativity is all about exploration and playfulness. Don't be afraid to experiment, make mistakes, and have fun with the process. Approach your creative pursuits with a childlike sense of wonder and curiosity.

Use Art as a Tool for Reflection: Art can be a powerful tool for reflection and self-discovery. Consider creating an art journal where you can express your thoughts, feelings, and experiences through drawing, painting, or collage. Use your art as a way to explore your inner landscape and gain a deeper understanding of yourself.

23: ART AND CREATIVITY: FINDING STILLNESS IN EX-PRESSION

Engage in Collaborative Art: Collaborative art projects can be a great way to connect with others and tap into a sense of shared creativity. Consider joining a community art project, attending a painting party, or collaborating with friends or family members on a creative project.

Immerse Yourself in Art: Simply immersing yourself in art can be a powerful way to cultivate stillness. Visit art museums, attend concerts or theater performances, or watch a documentary about your favorite artist. Allow yourself to be moved and inspired by the art around you.

Incorporating art and creativity into your life can be a powerful way to cultivate stillness and tap into your innermost self. Whether you're a seasoned artist or a complete beginner, there are endless ways to explore your creativity and find meaning and purpose through art. By embracing the power of art and creativity, you can unlock your true potential and live a more fulfilling life in the modern world.

24: Music and Sound: Finding Stillness in Harmony

Introduction

In our fast-paced modern world, it's easy to become disconnected from our inner selves and feel overwhelmed by the constant noise and distractions around us. But what if we could use music and sound as a tool to reconnect with our inner stillness and find a sense of harmony and peace?

In this chapter, we'll explore the power of music and sound to help us cultivate stillness and inner peace. We'll look at how different types of music and sound can affect our mood and energy, and how we can use them intentionally to create a more harmonious and balanced life.

The Power of Music and Sound

Music and sound have been used for centuries to evoke different emotions and moods. From the calming sounds of nature to the energizing beat of a drum, music and sound have the power to affect our physical, emotional, and spiritual states.

Research has shown that listening to music can have a pos-

itive impact on our mental health and well-being. It can reduce stress, anxiety, and depression, and improve our mood
and quality of life. Music can also help us relax and unwind,
which is essential for cultivating inner stillness and peace.

Different Types of Music and Their Effects

Not all music is created equal when it comes to promoting
stillness and inner peace. Some types of music can actually
increase stress and anxiety, while others can help us relax
and feel more grounded.

Here are some examples of different types of music and
their effects:

Classical Music: Classical music is often associated with relaxation and calm. Studies have shown that listening to classical music can reduce stress and anxiety, lower blood pressure, and improve mood and cognitive function.

Nature Sounds: The sounds of nature, such as birds chirp-
ing or waves crashing, can have a calming effect on the
mind and body. Listening to nature sounds can help us feel
more connected to the earth and promote a sense of inner

peace.

Meditation Music: Music specifically designed for meditation can help us relax and focus our minds. It often includes
soft, repetitive sounds and rhythms that can induce a state
of deep relaxation and stillness.

Binaural Beats: Binaural beats are a type of sound therapy
that involves listening to two different frequencies in each
ear. This can create a sense of harmony and balance in the
brain, which can help us feel more centered and calm.

Heavy Metal: On the other end of the spectrum, heavy
metal music is often associated with high levels of energy
and aggression. While it may be enjoyable for some, it's not
ideal for promoting stillness and inner peace.

Using Music and Sound for Stillness

Now that we understand the power of music and sound and
how they can affect our mood and energy, let's explore how
we can use them intentionally to cultivate stillness and inner peace.

Create a Playlist: One way to use music intentionally is to

create a playlist of songs that promote relaxation and calm. This could include classical music, nature sounds, or meditation music. Play this playlist when you're feeling stressed or overwhelmed, or as part of your daily self-care routine.

Practice Mindful Listening: Instead of using music as background noise, try practicing mindful listening. Choose a song or piece of music that resonates with you, and listen to it with your full attention. Focus on the sounds, rhythms, and melodies, and let yourself become fully absorbed in the music. This can be a powerful way to cultivate stillness and inner peace.

Use Sound Healing: Sound healing is a form of therapy that uses different types of sound, such as singing bowls or tuning forks, to promote relaxation and healing. You can attend a sound healing session or practice it on your own using a sound healing tool.

Practice Chanting or Singing: Chanting or singing can be a powerful way to connect with our inner stillness and find a sense of harmony and peace. Whether you're singing in a choir, chanting mantras, or simply humming a tune, the act of vocalizing can help us release tension and connect with our breath.

Use Music as a Movement Meditation: Movement meditation is a form of meditation that involves moving the body in a mindful and intentional way. You can use music to guide your movement meditation, choosing songs or pieces of music that inspire you to move in a fluid and graceful way.

Attend Live Music Events: Attending live music events, such as concerts or festivals, can be a powerful way to connect with the energy of music and sound. When we're surrounded by live music, we can feel a sense of unity and connection with others, which can promote a sense of inner peace and stillness.

Conclusion

In a world that's filled with noise and distractions, music and sound can be a powerful tool for cultivating stillness and inner peace. By choosing the right type of music and using it intentionally, we can reduce stress, anxiety, and overwhelm, and find a deeper sense of harmony and balance in our lives.

24: MUSIC AND SOUND: FINDING STILLNESS IN HARMONY

Whether you're listening to classical music, chanting mantras, or attending a live music event, the power of music and sound is available to us all. So next time you're feeling stressed or disconnected, try using music and sound to help you find your inner stillness and unlock your true potential for a more fulfilling life in the modern world.

25: Ritual and Ceremony: Finding Stillness in Sacred Space

In our fast-paced modern world, it's easy to get caught up in the hustle and bustle of daily life. We're constantly bombarded with distractions, demands, and obligations that leave us feeling stressed, anxious, and overwhelmed. But amidst all this chaos, there's a powerful tool that can help us find stillness and inner peace: ritual and ceremony.

Ritual and ceremony have been a part of human culture since the beginning of time. From ancient indigenous traditions to modern religious practices, humans have recognized the power of creating sacred space and engaging in intentional actions to connect with something greater than themselves.

At their core, rituals and ceremonies are all about intention. They provide a container for us to focus our attention and energy on a specific purpose or goal, whether that's healing, transformation, connection, or gratitude. When we engage in ritual and ceremony, we're taking a break from the chaos of everyday life and stepping into a space of stillness and intentionality.

25: RITUAL AND CEREMONY: FINDING STILLNESS IN SACRED SPACE

One of the most powerful aspects of ritual and ceremony is the way they can help us connect with our own inner wisdom and intuition. When we slow down and create sacred space, we're able to tune in to our own inner guidance and access a deeper sense of knowing. This can be especially valuable when we're feeling lost, uncertain, or overwhelmed in our lives.

There are countless ways to create ritual and ceremony in your own life, and the possibilities are limited only by your imagination. Here are just a few ideas to get you started:

Create a daily ritual: One of the simplest ways to incorporate ritual into your life is to create a daily practice that helps you start your day with intention. This could be as simple as lighting a candle and setting an intention for the day ahead, or it could involve a more elaborate practice like meditation, yoga, or journaling.

Connect with nature: Spending time in nature is a powerful way to connect with the sacred and tap into your own inner wisdom. Consider creating a ritual around a daily walk in the woods, or planning a camping trip that includes a ceremony to honor the natural world.

25: RITUAL AND CEREMONY: FINDING STILLNESS IN SACRED SPACE

Celebrate milestones and transitions: Whether it's a birthday, a graduation, a wedding, or the changing of the seasons, creating a ceremony to mark a significant milestone or transition can help you find closure and move forward with intention. This could involve lighting candles, creating an altar, sharing stories or poems, or simply spending time in quiet reflection.

Honor your ancestors: Connecting with your ancestors can be a powerful way to tap into your own lineage and find a sense of grounding and connection. Consider creating a ritual around visiting a family cemetery or ancestral homeland, or simply lighting a candle and offering prayers or gratitude to those who have come before you.

Connect with a community: Engaging in ritual and ceremony with others can be a powerful way to deepen your sense of connection and belonging. Consider joining a spiritual community or creating a group of like-minded individuals who gather regularly to share their intentions and support each other's growth.

Regardless of the specific form your ritual and ceremony takes, the most important thing is to approach it with intention and openness. By creating a sacred space and engaging in intentional actions, you can tap into the power of stillness and connect with your own inner wisdom and resilience. In a world that often feels chaotic and overwhelming, ritual and ceremony offer a path to greater peace, clarity, and connection.

26: The Wisdom of Stillness: Lessons from Spiritual Traditions

Introduction:

In our fast-paced and constantly changing world, it's easy to get caught up in the rush and lose touch with our inner selves. We often find ourselves running on autopilot, moving from one task to another without taking a moment to pause, reflect, and simply be. This is where the power of stillness comes in.

Stillness is the art of being present in the moment and embracing the quietness within. It's about slowing down, finding inner peace, and connecting with our deepest selves. And while stillness is a universal human experience, it has been emphasized and celebrated in many spiritual traditions throughout history. In this chapter, we'll explore some of the wisdom and lessons from various spiritual traditions that can guide us in cultivating stillness in our daily lives.

Lesson 1: Zen Buddhism and the Art of Mindfulness

Zen Buddhism is a spiritual tradition that originated in China and later developed in Japan. One of the core principles of Zen Buddhism is mindfulness, which involves being fully present and aware of the current moment without judgment or distraction.

In the Zen tradition, meditation is used as a tool to cultivate mindfulness and stillness. By focusing on the breath and observing the sensations in the body, we can learn to quiet the mind and enter a state of deep relaxation and peace.

The key lesson from Zen Buddhism is that stillness is not something we achieve or acquire, but rather it's a natural state that already exists within us. By practicing mindfulness and meditation, we can tap into this inner stillness and cultivate a greater sense of calm and clarity in our daily lives.

Lesson 2: Taoism and the Power of Wu Wei

Taoism is a spiritual tradition that originated in ancient China and emphasizes the importance of living in harmony with nature and the natural flow of life. One of the key principles of Taoism is Wu Wei, which can be translated as "non-action" or "effortless action."

Wu Wei doesn't mean doing nothing, but rather it means acting in a way that's in alignment with the natural flow of life. By letting go of our attachments and desires, we can allow things to unfold naturally and effortlessly.

The lesson from Taoism is that stillness doesn't necessarily mean doing nothing, but rather it means doing what's necessary without unnecessary effort or resistance. By embracing the principle of Wu Wei, we can learn to live in harmony with the natural flow of life and cultivate a greater sense of ease and grace in our daily lives.

Lesson 3: Hinduism and the Practice of Yoga

Hinduism is an ancient spiritual tradition that originated in India and emphasizes the importance of self-realization and spiritual growth. One of the key practices in Hinduism is Yoga, which is a system of physical, mental, and spiritual practices designed to cultivate stillness and inner peace.

The practice of Yoga involves various physical postures (asanas), breathing techniques (pranayama), and meditation (dhyana) to help quiet the mind and connect with the inner self. By practicing Yoga regularly, we can cultivate a greater sense of physical and emotional balance and access a deeper level of stillness and inner peace.

The lesson from Hinduism is that stillness is not just a state of mind, but it's also a state of being. By practicing Yoga and other spiritual practices, we can align our body, mind, and spirit and tap into the infinite stillness and peace that exists within us.

Lesson 4: Christianity and the Practice of Contemplation

Christianity is a spiritual tradition that originated in the Middle East and emphasizes the importance of love, compassion, and spiritual growth. One of the key practices in Christianity is contemplation, which is a form of meditation that involves reflecting on the divine nature of God and the interconnectedness of all things.

Contemplation involves focusing the mind on a particular thought, image, or phrase and allowing it to penetrate deeply into the heart. By contemplating on the divine nature of God and the interconnectedness of all things, we can cultivate a greater sense of stillness, peace, and unity with all of creation.

The lesson from Christianity is that stillness is not just about individual self-realization, but it's also about connecting with the greater divine and realizing our interconnectedness with all of creation. By practicing contemplation and other spiritual practices, we can deepen our connection with the divine and cultivate a greater sense of love, compassion, and unity in our daily lives.

Lesson 5: Sufism and the Practice of Dhikr

Sufism is a spiritual tradition that originated in the Middle East and emphasizes the importance of spiritual purification and self-realization. One of the key practices in Sufism is Dhikr, which is a form of meditation that involves repeating the names of God or other spiritual phrases.

By repeating the names of God or other spiritual phrases, we can quiet the mind and connect with the divine presence within us. Dhikr is also a form of remembrance, reminding us of our true nature and our connection with the divine.

The lesson from Sufism is that stillness is not just about quieting the mind, but it's also about opening the heart to the divine presence within us. By practicing Dhikr and other spiritual practices, we can purify our hearts and minds and cultivate a deeper connection with the divine.

Conclusion:

The wisdom and lessons from these spiritual traditions remind us that stillness is not just a state of mind, but it's also a state of being. By cultivating stillness in our daily lives through mindfulness, Wu Wei, Yoga, contemplation, and Dhikr, we can tap into the infinite stillness and peace that exists within us and connect with the greater divine.

Stillness is not about escaping from the world, but rather it's about finding inner peace and clarity amidst the chaos and noise of modern life. It's about embracing the present moment and connecting with our deepest selves and the greater world around us.

By incorporating these timeless wisdom and practices into our daily lives, we can overcome stress, anxiety, and overwhelm and cultivate a deep sense of calm, clarity, and resilience. We can unlock our true potential and live a more fulfilling and meaningful life in the modern world.

27: Buddhism: Finding Stillness in Impermanence

Buddhism is one of the world's oldest religions, and it has been practiced for more than 2,500 years. It is a way of life that emphasizes the teachings of the Buddha, who lived in India in the 5th century BCE. The Buddha, also known as Siddhartha Gautama, was a prince who gave up his royal status to seek enlightenment and understand the nature of suffering. He discovered the Four Noble Truths and the Eightfold Path, which are the foundation of Buddhism.

One of the key teachings of Buddhism is the concept of impermanence. Impermanence refers to the idea that everything in the universe is constantly changing and in a state of flux. This includes our thoughts, emotions, and physical bodies, as well as the world around us. Nothing is permanent, and everything is subject to decay and eventual dissolution.

At first glance, the idea of impermanence may seem depressing or even frightening. After all, if everything is impermanent, what is the point of striving for anything? However, the Buddha saw impermanence as a liberating truth. He believed that by accepting the impermanence of all things, we can let go of our attachments and desires, and find freedom from suffering.

In Buddhism, the ultimate goal is to achieve enlightenment, which is a state of perfect wisdom and compassion. Enlightenment is achieved by following the Eightfold Path, which includes ethical conduct, mindfulness, and meditation.

Mindfulness is a key component of Buddhist practice. It involves being fully present and aware of our thoughts, feelings, and sensations in the present moment, without judgment or distraction. By practicing mindfulness, we can cultivate a deep sense of stillness and inner peace, even in the midst of chaos and uncertainty.

Meditation is another important aspect of Buddhist practice. There are many different types of meditation, but they all involve training the mind to focus and become more aware. By meditating regularly, we can learn to quiet the chatter of our thoughts and find a sense of calm and clarity.

One of the most well-known forms of Buddhist meditation is vipassana, or insight meditation. Vipassana involves observing the breath and bodily sensations, and becoming more aware of the impermanent and constantly changing nature of our experiences. Through vipassana practice, we can learn to see things as they really are, without the distortions of our own biases and judgments.

Another form of Buddhist meditation is metta, or loving-kindness meditation. Metta involves cultivating feelings of compassion and goodwill towards ourselves and others. By practicing metta, we can develop a greater sense of empathy and connection with all beings, and reduce the harmful effects of anger and resentment.

In addition to meditation and mindfulness, Buddhism also emphasizes the importance of ethical conduct. The Buddha taught the Five Precepts, which are guidelines for living a moral and virtuous life. The Five Precepts include refraining from killing, stealing, lying, sexual misconduct, and taking intoxicants. By following these precepts, we can cultivate a greater sense of integrity and harmony in our relationships with others.

Buddhism also offers a wealth of wisdom on topics such as suffering, attachment, and desire. The Buddha taught that suffering arises from our attachment to things that are impermanent and subject to change. By recognizing the impermanence of all things, we can let go of our attachments and find freedom from suffering.

The Buddha also taught that desire is the root of suffering. When we crave things that we don't have, or cling to things that we fear losing, we create a sense of dissatisfaction and unease. By cultivating contentment and gratitude for what we have, we can reduce our desires and find greater happiness and fulfillment.

Overall, Buddhism offers a comprehensive framework for finding stillness and inner peace in a world that can often feel chaotic and overwhelming. By embracing the impermanence of all things, practicing mindfulness and meditation, and living a virtuous life, we can cultivate a deep sense of calm, clarity, and resilience that can carry us through life's challenges.

One of the most powerful teachings in Buddhism is the concept of non-attachment. Non-attachment refers to the idea that we should not cling to things or people, but rather accept them as they are and let go of our expectations and desires. This can be a difficult practice, especially in a cul-

ture that often values material possessions, status, and relationships above all else.

However, by cultivating non-attachment, we can free
ourselves from the cycle of craving and suffering. We can
learn to appreciate the beauty and richness of life without
becoming attached to any particular outcome or experience.
This can lead to a deep sense of peace and contentment,
even in the midst of difficult circumstances.

Another important aspect of Buddhism is the emphasis on
community and service. The Buddha taught that we should
work to alleviate the suffering of others, and that we should
cultivate a spirit of generosity and compassion. By serving
others, we can develop a sense of purpose and meaning in
our lives, and connect with something greater than
ourselves.

Buddhism also offers a rich tradition of stories and parables
that illustrate the teachings of the Buddha. One of the most
famous stories is that of the Buddha and the mustard seed.
In this story, a woman comes to the Buddha seeking help
for her child, who has died. The Buddha tells the woman to
bring him a mustard seed from a home where no one has

ever died. The woman searches and searches, but is unable to find such a home. In the end, she realizes the universality of suffering and finds comfort in the Buddha's teachings.

Another famous story is that of the monkey and the hunter. In this story, a monkey is caught in a trap and is about to be killed by a hunter. The monkey manages to escape by offering the hunter a lesson in mindfulness. The monkey points out that the hunter will never be able to catch him again if he remains still and observes his surroundings with great focus and awareness. The hunter is amazed by the monkey's wisdom and lets him go.

These stories and parables serve as powerful reminders of the timeless wisdom of Buddhism, and the potential for stillness and inner peace in all of us. By incorporating the teachings and practices of Buddhism into our lives, we can unlock our true potential and find a deep sense of fulfillment and meaning.

In conclusion, Buddhism offers a comprehensive framework for finding stillness and inner peace in the midst of a fast-paced and often chaotic world. By embracing the impermanence of all things, practicing mindfulness and meditation, and living a virtuous life, we can cultivate a deep sense of calm, clarity, and resilience that can carry us through life's challenges. Whether we are seeking enlightenment, or simply looking for a way to find greater happiness and fulfillment, the teachings of Buddhism offer a timeless and powerful guide.

28: Hinduism: Finding Stillness in Divine Union

Hinduism is one of the oldest religions in the world, dating back thousands of years. It is a complex and diverse religion with a rich history, mythology, and philosophy. One of the central themes of Hinduism is the idea of divine union, or the merging of the individual self with the universal self. This concept is closely tied to the practice of yoga, which is a means of achieving spiritual and physical stillness through the control of the mind and body.

The word "yoga" comes from the Sanskrit root "yuj," which means "to yoke" or "to unite." In Hinduism, the ultimate goal of yoga is to achieve union with the divine, or Brahman. Brahman is the ultimate reality in Hinduism, the source of all existence and the ultimate truth. It is often described as an infinite, eternal, and unchanging consciousness that pervades all of creation.

In order to achieve union with Brahman, Hindus practice a variety of yoga techniques, including physical postures (asanas), breath control (pranayama), meditation (dhyana), and other spiritual practices. These practices are designed to quiet the mind, control the senses, and cultivate a deep sense of inner stillness and peace.

One of the most well-known types of yoga is Hatha Yoga, which is the physical practice of yoga. Hatha Yoga is characterized by a series of postures or asanas that are designed to stretch and strengthen the body, increase flexibility, and improve balance and coordination. By focusing on the breath and the physical sensations of the body, practitioners are able to quiet the mind and enter a state of stillness and meditation.

Another type of yoga is Kundalini Yoga, which is focused on awakening the dormant energy at the base of the spine and directing it upwards towards the crown of the head. This practice involves a combination of physical postures, breathing exercises, chanting, and meditation, and is designed to help practitioners access higher levels of consciousness and achieve spiritual enlightenment.

In addition to yoga, Hinduism also includes a number of other spiritual practices and disciplines that are designed to cultivate inner stillness and peace. One of these practices is meditation, which involves focusing the mind on a particular object or sound in order to quiet the mind and cultivate a sense of inner peace and stillness.

Another practice is bhakti yoga, which is the yoga of devotion. Bhakti yoga involves cultivating a deep sense of love and devotion towards a particular deity or divine figure, such as Krishna or Shiva. By focusing on the qualities of the divine, practitioners are able to let go of their ego and enter into a state of stillness and surrender.

Finally, Hinduism also includes a number of spiritual texts and teachings that are designed to provide guidance and inspiration to practitioners. One of the most well-known of these texts is the Bhagavad Gita, which is a dialogue between the warrior Arjuna and his charioteer Krishna on the battlefield of Kurukshetra. The Bhagavad Gita is a profound and timeless work that offers guidance on how to live a spiritual life in the midst of worldly obligations and challenges.

In conclusion, Hinduism offers a rich and diverse tradition of spiritual practices and teachings that are designed to help practitioners cultivate inner stillness and peace. Whether through the physical practice of yoga, the discipline of meditation, the devotion of bhakti yoga, or the study of spiritual texts, Hindus have long recognized the importance of stillness and inner peace in achieving spiritual fulfillment and living a fulfilling life in the modern world.

29: Taoism: Finding Stillness in Harmony with Nature

Introduction

In today's fast-paced and technologically-driven world, finding moments of stillness can be challenging. We are constantly bombarded with stimuli, and the pressure to always be "on" can make it difficult to quiet our minds and find peace. Taoism offers a unique perspective on stillness and how we can cultivate it in our lives. In this chapter, we will explore the principles of Taoism and how they can help us find stillness and harmony with nature.

The Principles of Taoism

Taoism is a philosophical and spiritual tradition that originated in China over 2,000 years ago. At its core, Taoism emphasizes the importance of living in harmony with nature and finding balance in all aspects of life. The central concept in Taoism is the Tao, which can be translated as "the way" or "the path." The Tao is the natural order of the universe, and it is believed that by following it, we can live in harmony with ourselves, others, and the world around us.

29: TAOISM: FINDING STILLNESS IN HARMONY WITH NATURE

One of the key principles of Taoism is the idea of wu-wei, which can be translated as "non-action" or "effortless action." Wu-wei is the practice of acting in accordance with the Tao, without forcing or pushing things. Instead, it is about flowing with the natural rhythms of life and allowing things to unfold naturally. By practicing wu-wei, we can reduce stress and anxiety and find more peace and stillness in our lives.

Another important principle of Taoism is the idea of yin and yang. Yin and yang are complementary opposites that exist in all things. Yin represents the feminine, passive, and receptive aspects of life, while yang represents the masculine, active, and assertive aspects. It is believed that by balancing yin and yang in our lives, we can find greater harmony and stillness.

Cultivating Stillness in Taoism

In Taoism, stillness is not just a physical state but a state of mind. It is about finding inner calm and peace amidst the chaos of the world. There are several practices and techniques that Taoists use to cultivate stillness, including:

29: TAOISM: FINDING STILLNESS IN HARMONY WITH NATURE

Meditation: Meditation is a central practice in Taoism. It is a way to quiet the mind and connect with the Tao. Taoist meditation often involves focusing on the breath or on specific points in the body, such as the dantian (the energy center in the lower abdomen).

Nature observation: Taoists believe that nature is a reflection of the Tao and that by observing nature, we can learn valuable lessons about stillness and harmony. Spending time in nature, whether it is going for a walk in the woods or watching the sunrise, can help us connect with the natural rhythms of the world and find greater peace and stillness.

Tai chi and qigong: Tai chi and qigong are practices that involve slow, flowing movements and deep breathing. These practices are believed to help balance the body's energy and promote stillness and relaxation.

The Benefits of Stillness in Taoism

Finding stillness in Taoism has numerous benefits for our physical, mental, and emotional well-being. Some of the key benefits include:

Reduced stress and anxiety: By cultivating stillness, we can reduce the amount of stress and anxiety we experience in our lives. We can learn to let go of the things we cannot control and focus on the present moment.

Increased clarity and focus: Stillness allows us to quiet our minds and focus on what is truly important. It can help us see things more clearly and make better decisions.

Greater resilience: When we cultivate stillness, we become more resilient to the challenges of life. We learn to adapt to change and find peace even in difficult situations.

Conclusion

In a world that is constantly moving and changing, finding moments of stillness can be a powerful tool for finding inner peace and cultivating a deep sense of harmony with nature. Taoism offers a unique perspective on stillness and provides us with practical techniques and timeless wisdom to help us find stillness in our lives.

By embracing the principles of Taoism and practicing meditation, nature observation, tai chi, and qigong, we can reduce stress and anxiety, increase clarity and focus, and build greater resilience. Ultimately, finding stillness allows us to live more fulfilling and satisfying lives, connecting us to the natural world and helping us find a sense of purpose and meaning in our existence.

As we navigate the challenges and complexities of modern life, may we remember the wisdom of Taoism and take the time to cultivate stillness in our lives, finding peace, harmony, and fulfillment along the way.

30: Christianity: Finding Stillness in Surrender

In the modern world, people are constantly seeking ways to find peace, calm, and stillness in their lives. With so much stress, anxiety, and overwhelm, it can be difficult to find a sense of inner peace and contentment. However, for many people, their faith provides a source of comfort and strength in times of difficulty. Christianity, in particular, has a rich history of teachings and practices that can help individuals find stillness in surrender.

Surrender is often seen as a negative concept in our culture. We prize independence, self-sufficiency, and control. Surrender, on the other hand, implies giving up control and admitting our own limitations. However, in Christianity, surrender is not a sign of weakness, but rather a sign of strength. Surrendering to God and trusting in His plan can bring a deep sense of peace and contentment.

One of the key teachings of Christianity is the idea of surrendering oneself to God. This concept is central to many religious practices, including prayer, meditation, and contemplation. By surrendering oneself to God, one can let go of worries and fears, and trust in a higher power to guide and protect them. This can be a powerful tool for finding stillness in the midst of a chaotic world.

In addition to surrender, Christianity offers many other practices and teachings that can help individuals find stillness and peace. For example, meditation and contemplation are often used in Christian traditions to help individuals connect with God and find inner peace. By focusing on a particular scripture or prayer, individuals can quiet their minds and enter into a state of stillness and contemplation.

Another powerful tool for finding stillness in Christianity is the practice of gratitude. By cultivating a spirit of thankfulness, individuals can shift their focus away from their problems and worries, and instead focus on the good things in their lives. This can bring a sense of peace and contentment, even in the midst of difficult circumstances.

Finally, Christianity also offers the practice of forgiveness as a way to find stillness and inner peace. Holding onto anger, resentment, and bitterness can be a major source of stress and anxiety. By practicing forgiveness, individuals can release these negative emotions and find a sense of peace and freedom.

30: CHRISTIANITY: FINDING STILLNESS IN SUR-RENDER

Overall, Christianity offers a rich tradition of teachings and practices that can help individuals find stillness in surrender. By surrendering oneself to God, cultivating a spirit of gratitude, practicing meditation and contemplation, and practicing forgiveness, individuals can find a deep sense of peace and contentment in their lives. In a world that is often chaotic and stressful, these practices can be a powerful tool for finding stillness and inner peace.

31: Judaism: Finding Stillness in Contemplation

Judaism is one of the world's oldest and most influential religions, with a rich history and a diverse set of beliefs and practices. At its core, Judaism is a religion of contemplation, emphasizing the importance of introspection, meditation, and prayer as a means of connecting with God and achieving inner peace. In this chapter, we will explore how Judaism can help us find stillness through contemplation, and how we can apply these teachings in our modern lives.

The Importance of Contemplation in Judaism

In Judaism, the practice of contemplation is deeply ingrained in both the religious and cultural traditions of the faith. From the teachings of the Talmud and the Kabbalah to the practice of meditation and prayer, the pursuit of stillness and inner peace has been a central theme throughout Jewish history.

One of the most fundamental aspects of Jewish contemplation is the concept of Hitbodedut, which roughly translates to "self-seclusion" or "self-isolation." This practice involves setting aside a specific period of time each day for quiet reflection and introspection, allowing one to connect with God and gain a deeper understanding of oneself.

In Hitbodedut, practitioners often retreat to a quiet place, such as a forest or a secluded room, to meditate and contemplate. This practice is seen as a way of finding inner stillness, as it allows one to disconnect from the distractions and noise of the outside world and focus on the present moment.

Another important aspect of Jewish contemplation is the practice of Heshbon Hanefesh, or "accounting of the soul." This practice involves reflecting on one's actions, thoughts, and emotions, and assessing whether they align with one's values and beliefs. Through Heshbon Hanefesh, practitioners can identify areas for growth and improvement, and work towards living a more fulfilling and purposeful life.

The Role of Prayer in Jewish Contemplation

In addition to Hitbodedut and Heshbon Hanefesh, prayer is also a central aspect of Jewish contemplation. In Judaism, prayer is not just a means of asking for God's blessings or expressing gratitude, but also a way of connecting with the divine and finding inner peace.

In Jewish prayer, there is a strong emphasis on mindfulness and intentionality. Practitioners are encouraged to focus on the words and the meaning behind them, rather than simply reciting them by rote. This can help one achieve a state of calm and clarity, and deepen one's connection with God.

One of the most famous Jewish prayers is the Shema, which is recited twice daily by observant Jews. The Shema is a declaration of faith in God, and a reminder of the importance of loving God with all one's heart, soul, and might. Reciting the Shema is seen as a way of connecting with God and finding inner peace, as it reminds one of the ultimate source of all goodness and love.

The Kabbalah: A Source of Wisdom for Jewish Contemplation

The Kabbalah is a mystical tradition within Judaism that explores the nature of God and the universe, and seeks to uncover the deeper meanings behind the religious texts and practices of Judaism. The teachings of the Kabbalah have been a source of inspiration for Jewish contemplatives for centuries, and continue to be studied and practiced by many today.

One of the key concepts in the Kabbalah is the idea of Ein Sof, or the infinite and boundless nature of God. Through contemplation and meditation on the concept of Ein Sof, practitioners can gain a deeper understanding of the divine, and connect with the infinite source of all creation.

Another important aspect of the Kabbalah is the practice of Tikkun Olam, or "repairing the world." This concept emphasizes the importance of living a life of purpose and service, and working towards creating a more just and compassionate world. By engaging in acts of kindness, generosity, and social justice, practitioners can not only improve the world around them, but also find greater meaning and fulfillment in their own lives.

Practical Techniques for Jewish Contemplation

While the concepts and practices of Jewish contemplation may seem abstract or esoteric, there are many practical techniques that can be used to cultivate stillness and inner peace in daily life. Here are a few examples:

Mindful breathing: Taking a few deep breaths and focusing on the sensation of air moving in and out of the body can be a simple but effective way to calm the mind and find stillness.

Chanting: Reciting a favorite prayer or mantra, either silently or aloud, can help quiet the mind and connect with the divine.

Journaling: Writing down one's thoughts and reflections can be a powerful way of practicing Heshbon Hanefesh and gaining insight into one's own thoughts and emotions.

Walking meditation: Taking a slow, mindful walk in nature or around the block can be a great way to connect with the present moment and find inner peace.

Gratitude practice: Taking a few moments each day to reflect on what one is grateful for can help cultivate a sense of contentment and appreciation for the blessings in one's life.

Conclusion

31: JUDAISM: FINDING STILLNESS IN CONTEMPLATION

Jewish contemplation offers a rich and diverse set of practices and teachings for finding stillness and inner peace in the modern world. Whether through Hitbodedut, prayer, or the wisdom of the Kabbalah, practitioners of Jewish contemplation can connect with the divine, gain insight into their own thoughts and emotions, and work towards creating a more just and compassionate world. By incorporating these practices into our daily lives, we can cultivate a deep sense of calm, clarity, and resilience, and unlock our true potential for a more fulfilling life.

32: Islam: Finding Stillness in Submission

Islam is a religion that emphasizes the importance of finding peace and stillness in submission to God. For Muslims, finding inner peace is not only a personal pursuit but a religious obligation. Islam is a way of life that offers practical guidance on how to live a fulfilling and meaningful life while remaining true to one's faith. In this chapter, we will explore how Islam teaches us to find stillness in submission to God and how this can help us overcome stress, anxiety, and overwhelm.

The foundation of Islam is the belief in one God, Allah, who is the creator and sustainer of the universe. Muslims believe that everything in the universe is under Allah's control, and everything happens according to His will. This belief gives Muslims a sense of peace and comfort, knowing that they are not alone in the world and that there is a purpose to their existence.

One of the most important concepts in Islam is the idea of surrender or submission to Allah's will. Muslims are called to submit their will to Allah and to trust in His plan for their lives. This surrender is not a passive act but an active one that requires constant effort and intention. Muslims are taught to seek Allah's guidance in all aspects of their lives and to trust that His plan is always for their ultimate good.

Prayer is one of the most important practices in Islam and is central to finding stillness in submission. Muslims are required to pray five times a day, which helps to establish a rhythm of worship and reflection throughout the day. Prayer is a physical and spiritual act that requires focus and concentration, helping Muslims to quiet their minds and find peace in the presence of Allah.

In addition to prayer, Muslims are also encouraged to engage in other acts of worship, such as fasting during Ramadan, giving charity, and performing the pilgrimage to Mecca. These acts of worship help to strengthen one's relationship with Allah and to cultivate a sense of inner peace and tranquility.

Islam also places a strong emphasis on community and the importance of supporting and caring for one another. Muslims are encouraged to build strong relationships with their fellow believers, to be kind and compassionate, and to help those in need. This sense of community provides a source of comfort and support during difficult times and can help to alleviate stress and anxiety.

Another important aspect of finding stillness in submission is the cultivation of virtues such as patience, gratitude, and forgiveness. Muslims are taught to be patient in the face of adversity, to be grateful for the blessings in their lives, and to forgive those who have wronged them. These virtues help to cultivate a sense of inner peace and resilience, enabling Muslims to overcome stress and adversity with grace and dignity.

Islamic teachings also offer practical advice on how to live a balanced and fulfilling life. Muslims are encouraged to take care of their physical, emotional, and spiritual well-being, to prioritize their relationships with family and friends, and to engage in meaningful work and activities. This holistic approach to life helps to promote a sense of balance and harmony, which is essential for finding inner peace and stillness.

In conclusion, Islam offers a comprehensive approach to finding stillness in submission to Allah. Through prayer, acts of worship, community, the cultivation of virtues, and a holistic approach to life, Muslims can overcome stress, anxiety, and overwhelm and cultivate a deep sense of calm, clarity, and resilience. By surrendering their will to Allah and trusting in His plan, Muslims can find inner peace and fulfillment in the modern world.

33: Shamanism: Finding Stillness in Connection with Spirit

Shamanism is an ancient practice that has been used for centuries to connect with the spirit world and access deeper levels of consciousness. While many people associate shamanism with indigenous cultures and tribal societies, the truth is that shamanic practices can be found in many different traditions and spiritual paths. In this chapter, we will explore the role of shamanism in finding stillness and inner peace, and how you can incorporate shamanic techniques into your own spiritual practice.

At its core, shamanism is a spiritual practice that involves connecting with the spirit world through the use of ritual, ceremony, and altered states of consciousness. The term "shaman" refers to a spiritual leader or practitioner who has the ability to connect with the spirit world and communicate with spiritual beings such as ancestors, animal spirits, and divine entities.

Shamanism is often associated with the use of hallucinogenic plants such as ayahuasca or peyote, but these substances are not necessary for shamanic practice. Many shamanic traditions use drumming, chanting, and other forms of repetitive sound or movement to enter into altered states of consciousness and connect with the spirit world.

One of the key principles of shamanism is the belief that everything in the natural world is alive and has its own spirit or energy. This includes plants, animals, rocks, and even inanimate objects. By connecting with these spirits, shamanic practitioners can gain insight and guidance, and can also receive healing and transformational experiences.

In order to connect with the spirit world, shamanic practitioners often engage in rituals or ceremonies that involve creating a sacred space and invoking spiritual allies or guides. This can involve setting up an altar, lighting candles or incense, and using sacred objects such as feathers, crystals, or herbs.

Once the sacred space has been created, the practitioner will enter into an altered state of consciousness through the use of repetitive sound or movement. This can involve drumming, chanting, dancing, or other forms of trance-inducing practices. The purpose of these practices is to quiet the mind and allow the practitioner to access deeper levels of consciousness and connect with the spirit world.

33: SHAMANISM: FINDING STILLNESS IN CONNECTION WITH SPIRIT

One of the most powerful aspects of shamanism is its ability to help us connect with our own inner wisdom and guidance. By accessing the spirit world, we can gain insight into our own lives and discover new ways of healing and transformation. Shamanic practices can help us overcome fears, self-doubt, and limiting beliefs, and can help us cultivate a sense of inner strength, resilience, and clarity.

If you are interested in incorporating shamanic practices into your own spiritual practice, there are many resources available to help you get started. You can attend workshops or retreats with experienced shamanic practitioners, or you can read books and articles on the subject. There are also many online communities and forums where you can connect with other shamanic practitioners and share your experiences.

Here are some basic steps you can follow to begin your own shamanic practice:

Create a sacred space. Set up an altar or sacred area in your home where you can engage in shamanic practices. This can include lighting candles, burning incense, and using sacred objects such as feathers, crystals, or herbs.

Connect with your guides. Use repetitive sound or movement practices such as drumming, chanting, or dancing to
enter into an altered state of consciousness and connect
with your spiritual allies or guides. You can ask for guidance, insight, or healing, or simply be open to whatever
messages or experiences come through.

Cultivate stillness. After engaging in shamanic practices,
take time to be still and reflect on your experiences. Write
down any insights or messages you received, and try to integrate these into your daily life.

Practice regularly. Like any spiritual practice, shamanism
requires regular practice and commitment in order to see
results. Set aside time each day or week to engage in shamanic practices, and be consistent with your efforts.

Seek guidance from experienced practitioners. If you are
new to shamanism, it can be helpful to seek guidance from
experienced practitioners or teachers. Attend workshops or
retreats, or connect with online communities where you can
ask questions and receive support.

Honor the natural world. Shamanism is rooted in a deep respect and reverence for the natural world. Take time to connect with the earth, spend time in nature, and cultivate a sense of gratitude for the abundance and beauty of the natural world.

As you begin to incorporate shamanic practices into your own spiritual practice, you may notice a sense of inner peace, clarity, and resilience emerging within you. By connecting with the spirit world and accessing deeper levels of consciousness, you can overcome stress, anxiety, and overwhelm, and cultivate a deep sense of stillness and inner peace.

In addition to the practices outlined above, there are many shamanic tools and techniques that can be used to enhance your spiritual practice. These can include working with crystals, herbs, or other sacred objects, using divination tools such as tarot or oracle cards, and engaging in soul retrieval or other forms of energy healing.

Ultimately, the key to finding stillness and inner peace through shamanism is to cultivate a sense of openness, curiosity, and reverence for the natural world and the unseen realms of spirit. By connecting with our own inner wisdom

and the wisdom of the universe, we can unlock our true potential and discover a more fulfilling, peaceful, and joyful
way of living in the modern world.

34: Indigenous Wisdom: Finding Stillness in the Wisdom of the Ancestors

The wisdom of indigenous cultures has been passed down from generation to generation for thousands of years. These cultures have long understood the importance of stillness, and have developed various techniques to cultivate a deep sense of calm, clarity, and resilience. In this chapter, we will explore the wisdom of indigenous cultures and how it can help us find stillness in the modern world.

The indigenous peoples of the world have always had a deep connection with nature. They have learned to live in harmony with the natural world, and have developed spiritual practices that allow them to connect with the earth, the sky, and all living beings. This connection to nature is an essential part of their wisdom, and it can help us find stillness in our own lives.

One of the most important teachings of indigenous cultures is the importance of listening. They believe that we must learn to listen to the natural world and to our own inner voice. By listening deeply, we can develop a greater sense of awareness and understanding, and we can find stillness in the midst of the chaos of modern life.

Another important aspect of indigenous wisdom is the concept of interconnectivity. Indigenous cultures believe that all things are connected, and that we are all part of a larger whole. This understanding can help us find stillness by reminding us that we are not alone, and that we are part of something greater than ourselves.

Indigenous cultures have also developed various practices to help cultivate stillness. For example, many indigenous cultures practice meditation and mindfulness. They believe that by focusing their attention on their breath or on a particular object, they can quiet their minds and find a sense of peace.

Other indigenous practices include chanting, drumming, and dancing. These practices can help us connect with our bodies and with the natural world, and they can help us find stillness in the midst of movement and activity.

In addition to these practices, many indigenous cultures also use herbs and other natural remedies to promote physical and emotional well-being. These remedies can help us find stillness by promoting relaxation and reducing stress and anxiety.

One of the most important teachings of indigenous cultures is the importance of community. They believe that we are all connected, and that we must work together to create a better world. By cultivating strong relationships with others, we can find stillness in the midst of social interaction and collaboration.

Indigenous cultures also teach us the importance of gratitude. They believe that by being grateful for what we have, we can find stillness in the midst of difficulty and challenge. Gratitude helps us focus on the positive aspects of our lives, and it can help us find a sense of peace and contentment.

Finally, indigenous cultures teach us the importance of honoring our ancestors. They believe that our ancestors are still with us, and that we can learn from their wisdom and guidance. By connecting with our ancestors, we can find stillness by tapping into the deep reservoir of knowledge and understanding that they have left for us.

34: INDIGENOUS WISDOM: FINDING STILLNESS IN THE WISDOM OF THE ANCESTORS

In conclusion, the wisdom of indigenous cultures offers a powerful framework for finding stillness in the modern world. By connecting with nature, listening deeply, practicing mindfulness and meditation, cultivating community, and honoring our ancestors, we can develop a deep sense of calm, clarity, and resilience. These practices can help us overcome stress, anxiety, and overwhelm, and can lead us to a more fulfilling life.

35: The Power of Stillness: Integrating Your Practice into Daily Life

The practice of stillness, also known as mindfulness or meditation, is a powerful tool for cultivating a deep sense of calm, clarity, and resilience in the midst of the chaos of modern life. It can help us to overcome stress, anxiety, and overwhelm, and unlock our true potential by allowing us to tap into our inner wisdom and intuition.

But while the benefits of stillness are clear, many people struggle to integrate their practice into their daily lives. In this chapter, we will explore some practical techniques and timeless wisdom to help you make stillness a part of your daily routine, so you can reap the benefits of a more fulfilling life.

Creating a Stillness Practice

The first step in integrating stillness into your daily life is to create a consistent practice. This can be as simple as setting aside a few minutes each day to sit in silence and focus on your breath. Over time, you can gradually increase the amount of time you spend in stillness, and explore different techniques to find what works best for you.

One helpful technique for establishing a consistent practice is to set aside a dedicated space in your home where you can meditate or practice stillness. This could be a small corner of a room, a meditation cushion or bench, or even a dedicated room or studio. Having a designated space can help to create a sense of sacredness and intentionality around your practice.

Another helpful technique is to set a specific time each day for your practice. This could be first thing in the morning, before bed, or during a lunch break. By creating a regular routine, you are more likely to stick with your practice over the long term.

Incorporating Stillness into Daily Life

While it is important to have a dedicated practice, the true power of stillness lies in its ability to permeate every aspect of our lives. By bringing a sense of presence and awareness to our daily activities, we can transform even the most mundane tasks into opportunities for growth and learning.

35: THE POWER OF STILLNESS: INTEGRATING YOUR PRACTICE INTO DAILY LIFE

One way to integrate stillness into your daily life is to practice mindfulness throughout the day. This means bringing your full attention to whatever you are doing in the present moment, whether it is washing dishes, taking a walk, or having a conversation with a loved one. By focusing on your senses and your breath, you can stay grounded in the present moment and cultivate a sense of calm and clarity, even in the midst of a busy day.

Another way to integrate stillness into your daily life is to set intentions for each day. This could be as simple as setting an intention to be kind to yourself and others, or to focus on gratitude and appreciation. By setting intentions, you are creating a sense of purpose and direction for your day, and cultivating a mindset of mindfulness and intentionality.

Practical Techniques for Stillness

While there are many different techniques for practicing stillness, some of the most effective include:

Breathwork: Focusing on your breath is a simple yet powerful way to cultivate stillness and calm. By taking slow, deep breaths and focusing on the sensation of the breath moving in and out of your body, you can quiet your mind and connect with your inner wisdom.

Body Scan: This technique involves scanning your body from head to toe, and noticing any sensations or areas of tension. By bringing awareness to your body in this way, you can release physical tension and connect with your body's natural wisdom and intuition.

Guided Meditation: Listening to a guided meditation can be a helpful way to quiet your mind and cultivate stillness. There are many different types of guided meditations available, from body scans to visualizations to affirmations, so you can choose one that resonates with you.

Walking Meditation: This technique involves walking slowly and mindfully, focusing on the sensation of your feet touching the ground and the movement of your body. This can be a helpful way to cultivate stillness while also getting some gentle exercise and fresh air.

Mantra Meditation: This technique involves repeating a word or phrase, such as "peace" or "love," in your mind. By focusing on the mantra and repeating it with each breath, you can quiet your mind and connect with a sense of inner calm and clarity.

Gratitude Practice: Practicing gratitude is a powerful way to cultivate stillness and shift your focus from what is lacking to what you already have. One simple way to practice gratitude is to write down three things you are grateful for each day, or simply take a few moments each morning or evening to reflect on the things in your life that bring you joy and fulfillment.

Timeless Wisdom for Stillness

While there are many practical techniques for cultivating stillness, there is also a wealth of timeless wisdom that can help us to deepen our practice and connect with our inner wisdom and intuition. Here are a few key principles to keep in mind as you integrate stillness into your daily life:

Non-judgment: One of the core principles of stillness is non-judgment. This means cultivating a sense of acceptance and compassion for yourself and others, without judgment or criticism. By practicing non-judgment, you can cultivate a sense of peace and connection with yourself and the world around you.

Letting go: Another key principle of stillness is letting go of attachment and expectations. This means releasing the need to control or manipulate outcomes, and instead trusting in the natural flow of life. By letting go, you can cultivate a sense of surrender and trust, and open yourself up to new possibilities and opportunities.

Presence: Stillness is all about being present in the moment, and cultivating a sense of awareness and mindfulness. By bringing your full attention to the present moment, you can connect with your inner wisdom and intuition, and tap into the deeper truths that lie within.

Compassion: Finally, stillness is about cultivating compassion and kindness towards yourself and others. By practicing compassion, you can cultivate a sense of connection and empathy, and create a more loving and harmonious world.

In conclusion, integrating stillness into your daily life can be a powerful way to unlock your true potential and find inner peace and fulfillment in the midst of the chaos of modern life. By creating a consistent practice, incorporating stillness into your daily activities, and exploring practical techniques and timeless wisdom, you can cultivate a deep sense of calm, clarity, and resilience that will serve you well in all aspects of your life.

36: Conclusion: Embracing Stillness as a Path to Fulfillment and Freedom

In today's fast-paced world, it's easy to feel overwhelmed and stressed out. We're bombarded with information from all angles, and it seems like there's always something that needs our attention. In the midst of all this chaos, it can be hard to find a sense of inner peace and calm. But what if I told you that there was a way to harness the power of stillness to overcome stress, anxiety, and overwhelm, and cultivate a deep sense of fulfillment and freedom?

In this comprehensive guide, we've explored the many ways in which stillness can transform your life. From mindfulness meditation and breathwork to yoga and nature immersion, we've covered a wide range of techniques and practices that can help you tap into the power of stillness and find greater peace and clarity in your daily life.

But stillness is more than just a set of techniques or practices. It's a way of being that requires a deep inner shift in how we approach ourselves and the world around us. It requires us to slow down, tune in, and cultivate a greater awareness of our thoughts, emotions, and physical sensations.

When we embrace stillness as a path to fulfillment and freedom, we open ourselves up to a world of new possibilities. We become more resilient in the face of stress and adversity, and we're better able to navigate the challenges that life throws our way. We find a greater sense of purpose and meaning, and we're able to connect more deeply with ourselves and others.

But how do we actually go about embracing stillness in our daily lives? The first step is to recognize that stillness is not something that we can achieve or attain. It's already present within us, waiting to be uncovered and cultivated. All we need to do is create the space and conditions for it to emerge.

One of the most effective ways to create this space is through mindfulness meditation. By sitting in stillness and observing our thoughts and sensations without judgment, we can cultivate a greater awareness of our inner landscape and learn to disidentify from our thoughts and emotions. This can help us develop a greater sense of inner calm and equanimity, even in the face of stress and difficulty.

Another powerful way to cultivate stillness is through breathwork. By focusing our attention on our breath and using specific techniques to regulate our breathing, we can tap into the power of the parasympathetic nervous system and activate our body's natural relaxation response. This can help us release tension and stress, and enter a state of deep relaxation and peace.

Yet another way to cultivate stillness is through yoga. By practicing yoga poses and movements with awareness and intention, we can create a sense of harmony and balance within our bodies and minds. This can help us release physical and emotional tension, and tap into a deeper sense of calm and centeredness.

Of course, there are many other ways to cultivate stillness as well, from spending time in nature to engaging in creative pursuits like painting or writing. The key is to find the practices and techniques that resonate with you personally, and to make a commitment to incorporating them into your daily life.

36: CONCLUSION: EMBRACING STILLNESS AS A PATH TO FULFILLMENT AND FREEDOM

Ultimately, the journey towards stillness is a lifelong process, and there will be ups and downs along the way. But with patience, persistence, and a willingness to explore and experiment, you can tap into the power of stillness and unlock your true potential for fulfillment and freedom.

So I invite you to take the next step on this journey. Set aside some time each day to sit in stillness, to focus on your breath, or to engage in a practice that brings you a sense of peace and calm. Cultivate a sense of curiosity and openness, and be willing to let go of your preconceptions and expectations.

In doing so, you'll discover a world of new possibilities and experiences, and you'll begin to unlock the true potential of stillness in your life. You'll find that as you cultivate greater awareness and presence, you'll be better equipped to handle the challenges and stresses of daily life with greater ease and grace.

You may also find that as you deepen your connection with yourself, you begin to connect more deeply with others as well. As you tap into your own inner well of peace and calm, you'll radiate that energy out into the world around you, inspiring others to do the same.

But perhaps most importantly, as you embrace stillness as a path to fulfillment and freedom, you'll discover a deeper sense of purpose and meaning in your life. You'll begin to see that the journey towards stillness is not just about finding peace and tranquility in the moment, but about living a life that is aligned with your deepest values and aspirations.

So I encourage you to continue on this journey, to explore the many ways in which stillness can transform your life, and to cultivate a daily practice of presence and awareness. Remember that the path towards stillness is not a linear one, and that there will be times when you stumble and fall. But with patience, perseverance, and a commitment to your own growth and well-being, you can harness the power of stillness to create a life that is truly fulfilling and free.

In closing, I'd like to offer you a final thought. As you embark on this journey towards stillness, remember that you are not alone. There are countless others who are walking this path alongside you, each with their own unique challenges and aspirations. Together, we can support and inspire each other, sharing our insights and experiences along the way.

So take a deep breath, let go of any tension or stress, and embrace the stillness that is already present within you. Trust that as you continue on this path, you'll uncover new depths of wisdom and insight, and discover a life that is truly fulfilling and free.

Thank You

As we reach the end of this book, I want to say thanks for reading this book.

I want to get this information out to as many people as possible. If you found this book helpful, I would greatly appreciate you leaving me a review. This helps others find the book as well.

Disclaimer

This document is geared towards providing exact and reliable information in regards to the topic and issue covered. The publication is sold on the idea that the publisher is not required to render an accounting, officially permitted, or otherwise, qualified services. If advice is necessary, legal, financial, medical or professional, a practiced individual in the profession should be ordered.

This information is not presented by a financial or medical practitioner and is for entertainment, educational and informational purposes only. The content is not intended as a substitute for professional medical advice, diagnosis, or treatment. Always seek the advice of your physician or other qualified health care provider with any questions you may have regarding a medical condition. Never disregard professional medical advice or delay in seeking it because of something you have read.

The information provided herein is stated to be truthful and consistent, in that any liability, in terms of inattention or otherwise, by any usage or abuse of any policies, processes, or directions contained within is the solitary and utter responsibility of the recipient reader. Under no circumstances

DISCLAIMER

will any legal responsibility or blame be held against the publisher for any reparation, damages, or monetary loss due to the information herein, either directly or indirectly.

www.ingramcontent.com/pod-product-compliance
Lightning Source LLC
Chambersburg PA
CBHW060513130626
46553CB00002B/473